Disclaimer

The publisher of this book is by no way associated with the National Institute of Standards and Technology (NIST). The NIST did not publish this book. It was published by 50 page publications under the public domain license.

50 Page Publications.

Book Title: Data Exchange of Parametric CAD Models Using ISO 10303-108

Book Author: Junhwan Kim; Mike Pratt; Raj G. Iyer; Ram D. Sriram

Book Abstract: Modern CAD systems generate feature-based product shape models with parameterization and constraints. Until recently, standards for CAD data exchange among different CAD systems were restricted to the exchange of pure shape information. These standards ignored the parameters, constraints, features, and other elements of ? design intent? present in the model to be transferred. This paper suggests an implementational foundation for CAD data exchange with parametric information for the preservation of design intent, based on the use of newly published parts of the International Standard ISO 10303, which is informally known as STEP ? STandard for Exchange of Product model data. A case study is presented, which employs a hypothetical STEP application protocol (AP) using Parts 55, 108 and 111 of ISO 10303. A prototype translator based on this AP has been implemented and tested. The paper reports on the experience gained in parametric data exchange.

Citation: NIST Interagency/Internal Report (NISTIR) - 7433

Keyword: constraints;Data exchange;design intent;parameterization;parametric CAD models;STEP

NISTIR 7433

Data Exchange of Parametric CAD Models Using ISO 10303-108

Junwahn Kim
Michael J. Pratt
Raj Iyer
Ram Sriram

National Institute of Standards and Technology
Technology Administration, U.S. Department of Commerce

NISTIR 7433

Data Exchange of Parametric CAD Models Using ISO 10303-108

Junwahn Kim
Ram D. Sriram
Manufacturing Systems Integration Division
Manufacturing Engineering Laboratory

Michael J. Pratt
LMR Systems, Carlton
Bedford MK43 7LA, UK

Raj G. Iyer
TACOM, US Army
Warren, MI 48397

July 2007

U.S. Department of Commerce
Carlos M. Gutierrez, Secretary

Technology Administration
Robert Cresanti, Under Secretary of Commerce for Technology

National Institute of Standards and Technology
William Jeffrey, Director

DATA EXCHANGE OF PARAMETRIC CAD MODELS
USING ISO 10303-108

Junhwan Kim[a], Michael J. Pratt[b], Raj G. Iyer[c] and Ram D. Sriram[a]

[a] National Institute of Standards & Technology (NIST), Gaithersburg, MD 20899, USA
[b] LMR Systems, Carlton, Bedford MK43 7LA, UK
[c] TACOM, US Army, Warren, MI 48397, USA
[Contact Person E-mail: mike@lmr.clara.co.uk]

ABSTRACT

Modern CAD systems generate feature-based product shape models with parameterization and constraints. Until recently, standards for CAD data exchange among different CAD systems were restricted to the exchange of pure shape information. These standards ignored the parameters, constraints, features, and other elements of 'design intent' present in the model to be transferred. This paper suggests an implementational foundation for CAD data exchange with parametric information for the preservation of design intent, based on the use of newly published parts of the International Standard ISO 10303, which is informally known as STEP – STandard for Exchange of Product model data. A case study is presented, which employs a hypothetical STEP application protocol (AP) using Parts 55, 108 and 111 of ISO 10303. A prototype translator based on this AP has been implemented and tested. The paper reports on the experience gained in parametric data exchange.

Key words: Data exchange, parametric CAD models, STEP, design intent, parameterization, constraints.

TABLE OF CONTENTS

1. INTRODUCTION

The exchange of CAD (Computer Aided Design) models between different CAD systems and to downstream applications has become very important to modern industry. Until recently, national and international CAD data exchange standards including ISO 10303, which is informally known as STEP – STandard for Exchange of Product model data [1,2,3], have been limited to transferring geometry. These standards have been incapable of handling parameters, constraints, design features and other 'design intent' data generated by modern CAD systems [4]. Most STEP translators can currently only transfer 'dumb' shape models encapsulating the final result of some constructional process, all information about that process being lost in the exchange. Essential elements of the lost information include:

1. *Construction history*: the procedure used to construct the shape model;
2. *Parameters*: variables associated with dimensional or other values in the model, providing an indication of what it is permissible to change; and
3. *Constraints*: relationships between parameter values or between geometric or topological elements of the model, specifying invariant characteristics in the model under editing operations, usually in the interests of maintaining product functionality during modification.

A new part of ISO 10303, Part 55 of the standard, formally referred to as ISO 10303-55 [5], has recently been published. Its title is, 'Procedural and hybrid representation' and it provides for the transfer of construction history information. A recently published companion document, ISO 10303-108 ('Parameterization and constraints for explicit geometric product models') [6], is intended to provide means for the capture and transfer of the second and third classes of information referred to above. A third STEP resource document, ISO 10303-111 ('Elements for the procedural modeling of solid shapes') [7] provides representations for what are commonly known as 'design features.' It will be published by ISO before the end of 2007. The transfer of design intent information using Parts 55, 108 and 111 of STEP will allow the intuitive editing of a model in a receiving system after it has been transferred, a capability which is not available with the 'dumb' models resulting from earlier STEP exchanges. In industry, much time is currently spent by CAD system users in trying to reconstruct the lost design intent in exchanged models. Use of the new STEP capabilities will avoid the need for such non-productive activity [8].

Before proceeding further, some explanation should be given regarding the representation of 'design features' in ISO 10303-111. Strictly speaking, a 'feature' or 'form feature' is a shape element that has engineering significance for some phase in the product life-cycle. However, CAD systems generate only the shape element, with no associated engineering semantics. The functional significance of any created form element is doubtless present in the mind of the designer using a CAD system, but this information is not currently captured in the design process, and no plausible means of doing so has yet emerged despite several years of research directed to that end. Thus the shape configurations defined in ISO 10303-111 are not form features in the accepted sense.

By contrast, other parts of ISO 10303, notably ISO 10303-214, ISO 10303-224 and other manufacturing-oriented parts, define form features with associated semantics for specific application domains. They adopt the viewpoint that the geometry of a form feature is a subregion of the boundary of a full part model. But the shape elements defined in ISO 10303-111 are possibly only ephemeral. They are initially regarded as idealized shapes, which may lose their ideal form when installed on a part model, and may then be further modified or even deleted from the model as a result of subsequent constructional operations. It is therefore not appropriate to model them as aspects of the shape of the final model. For that and other reasons it was decided to regard the shape elements defined in ISO 10303-111 in a similar light to those defined in ISO 10303-42, the basic ISO 10303 geometry/topology resource, in particular the swept solids and boolean combinations specified there. Indeed, some of the entities defined in ISO 10303-111 are directly subtyped from ISO 10303-42 entities.

This paper provides some theoretical foundations for parametric data exchange in current and future CAD systems, and uses these to review the new parts of the STEP standard. The technical goal is preservation and transmission of design intent information during a model transfer so that the model can be edited in the receiving system as though it had originally been created there. The paper also reports on experience gained from the development and use of a prototype translator using the newly available ISO 10303 capabilities.

Some of the problems observed in developing the translators, which read and write information through the applications programming interfaces (APIs) of the CAD systems used in the tests, are as follows:

(a) Semantic differences: The elements of information differ among CAD systems. For example, a single constraint from one system may need to be mapped to two or more constraints in another. Semantic differences also exist at a deeper level. A dimension in CAD System A (the sending system) may not correspond to the notion of a dimension as defined in ISO 10303-108. In such a case the semantics of the data may need to be inferred not from the CAD system data structure but from the general modeling context. In the case of design features, the mapping from a feature in CAD System A to a neutral (STEP) feature, and from the neutral feature to a feature in CAD System B (the receiving system) is not always one-to-one. Additional information may need to be transferred, possibly including geometry, constraints and dimensions, to accommodate the difference in feature definitions between systems. Furthermore, it is sometimes necessary to convert some of the information implicit in the feature definition of System A to explicit logical or dimensional constraints and parameters in the STEP representation, to avoid potential information loss. If procedural (construction history) information is available from the sending system, it may in some cases be used to deduce explicit information that can be transferred to the receiving system.

(b) Implicitly created information: In many cases, parameters and constraints are not created explicitly by the designer, but arise implicitly through the use of constructional operations, where their effect is built in [9]. How can a translator determine what has been created by the designer and what has been created automatically by the system? How can it deduce explicit information needed by the receiving system if that information only exists implicitly in the sending system? How can we control the automatically generated information in a reconstruction of a model following a transfer? The presence or absence of such information influences the constructional procedure, so that apparently identical procedures do not guarantee that the same model is generated in different CAD systems.

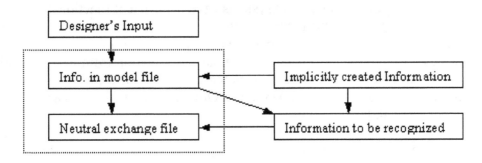

Fig.1 Information flow during parametric data transmission

(c) Design rationale: It has been pointed out by Ohtaka that a constructional history, even if it can be transmitted effectively, may be difficult to work with in a receiving system [10]. One reason for this is because the history alone lacks any information about the designer's motivation in choosing a particular design methodology (this motivation is generally referred to as *design rationale*). In its absence, it may be hard to modify the model in accordance with the designer's original approach. Another reason is that the construction history of a complex model may be large and have many embedded levels of detail, and consequently be difficult to understand and modify. Both difficulties could be overcome through the provision of design rationale information with the construction history transfer. However, no effective method has yet been found for capturing such information automatically during the design process, although several academic projects have made attempts to accomplish this. The best that can be done at present is to make provision for the insertion of design rationale in text form at appropriate points in the history. That will require the designer to input the text during the design process (possibly by speech recognition rather than via the keyboard). Problems may still result from differences in the way that designers view and describe the design process.

(d) Granularity of processing: There are differences between CAD systems in the complexity of the geometric structures that can be created by a single operation. We refer to such differences in terms of *granularity*. An operation with coarse granularity in one system may need to be mapped onto a sequence of operations with finer granularity in another. For example, some systems allow the creation of under-constrained sketches or features, which allow later fine-tuning of the model in terms of lower-level operations. On the other hand, other systems allow only the creation of fully constrained constructs, possibly through the use of default options. The identification of such defaults and their appropriate capture in an exchange file proves to be difficult.

(e) Numerical Accuracy: Differences in the internal numerical accuracy of CAD systems was a major early cause of problems in the STEP-based exchange of B-rep models [11]. For example, two points that are judged to be coincident by one system may have separate locations in another. This can lead to inconsistency between the geometry and the topology of a model in an exchange from a system with loose numerical tolerances to a system with more stringent criteria. In ten years of use of AP203 for the exchange of B-reps, techniques have been developed that greatly reduce the severity of this problem, but it is necessary to examine the potential impact of the additional geometric accuracy problems that will arise in parametric data exchange.

(f) Implementational issues: Some CAD systems have insufficient functionality in their APIs to allow the input and output of all the required information. A report on the recent PDES Inc. CHAPS project, for example, mentions a case where constraint information cannot be accessed [12]. Sometimes it is possible to deduce the necessary information from what is available, for example in the determination of the reference elements in geometric constraints whose identifiers are not explicitly provided by most CAD systems. Other similar difficulties are described in a paper by Rappoport et al. [13].

In this paper, the methodology for the exchange of parametric models using ISO 10303-108 is discussed under several sub-headings:

(1) Classification: A parametric model differs significantly from a 'traditional' B-rep model. In B-rep model exchange (for example, using AP203 of ISO 10303 [14]), the information transferred primarily concerns the geometry and topology of the 'final' model as displayed on the CAD system screen. A parametric model contains a much wider class of information elements. We therefore need to define and classify the types of information required for the exchange of parametric models, and to use the classification to analyze the types of information available in the model repository of the sending system. The latter varies between systems, and is not necessarily sufficient to support the desired exchange. Classification is discussed in section 3.

(2) Structuring: For the most effective mapping of information between systems, a set of model elements in the sending system should be mapped onto a set of (possibly different) elements in the receiving system that has the same number of parametric degrees of freedom. Ideally, the set would consist of a single feature definition in both systems, but CAD system features often have more complex semantics than the features defined in ISO 10303-111, or vice versa. In the first case, a STEP feature will have to be transmitted together with some lower-level supporting elements, to make up the required number of degrees of freedom and avoid information loss. Differences between the systems of internal identifiers in CAD systems and the identification mechanism used in ISO 10303 exchange files have some bearing on this issue, and these will be analyzed later in the paper. Structuring is discussed in section 4.

(3) Interoperability: This topic is concerned with the resolution of semantic differences between similar constructs in different CAD systems. It also covers the problem of incompatible numerical tolerances mentioned above. The achievement of semantic and numerical interoperability will ensure the maximum preservation of model integrity and design intent in the exchange of CAD models. Interoperability is discussed in section 5.

Organization of the paper. Section 2 provides a literature review of various projects aimed at exchanging CAD models with design history and parametric data. Section 3 discusses the classification of information concerning parameters, constraints, and geometry. This classification will allow us to better understand the scope of different algorithms. Section 4 deals with a hierarchical information structure for dimensions, constraints, and parameters. Doing so aids in defining *units of creation*, which are used in the design and implementation of our translators. Section 5 discusses the interoperability of parameters, constraints, and selected geometric elements. Several guidelines for information preservation are provided. Section 6 presents an implementation of the translator, along with several case studies. Section 7 summarizes our work and explores future research.

2. LITERATURE REVIEW

Most early work on data exchange of 3D CAD models, whether using formal (IGES, STEP) or *de facto* (DXF, SAT) standards, focused on the final geometry of the model. [1] For example, the STEP application protocol AP203 [14] allows the transfer of boundary representation (B-rep) and closely related types of model, including assemblies of such models. The difference between AP203-based translation and the approach described in this paper is that we can now effectively transfer parameterized families of models, defined in terms of features, dimensions, constraints and construction history information — in short, the types of model generated by modern CAD systems. This enables the preservation of the design intent in the original model.

An early suggestion for a method of exchanging CAD models in terms of their construction history was made by Hoffmann and Juan [15]. Their EREP (editable representation) was a specification for the representation of sequential feature-based design processes. It supported parameterization and constraints, and was the subject of a trial implementation.

Another project aimed at moving beyond the exchange of pure geometric models was the PDES Inc. project ENGEN ('Enabling Next GENeration design') project [16]. This used representations based on STEP methodology [2,3]. It concentrated mainly on the exchange of geometric constraints and demonstrated the exchange of constrained 2D profile data. The ENGEN Data Model also made very limited provision for procedural entities representing constructional elements, for instance **construct_circle_three_points**. The new STEP resource ISO 10303-112, recently published as an International Standard, defines a wider range of entities of this type, corresponding to the common capabilities of major modern CAD systems.

It is not necessary to capture the entire sequence of operations used by a designer, because not all operations are related to product shape. Examples of non-shape operations include the assignment of colors to elements of the shape model, or visualization commands (rotations of the model, zoom commands, etc.) [17]. There is also the problem that, if every detail of the design sequence is captured the resulting file will include all the errors made by the designer, and all the resulting recovery procedures, whereas what is needed is usually the direct procedure leading to the final model.

In a general sense the word 'constraint', especially in non-geometric context, may relate to restrictions on diverse issues such as material properties, manufacturing processes, and working environments [8], but we consider only geometric constraints. Bettig and Shah [18] proposed a standard set of geometric constraints for parametric modeling and data exchange. They defined explicit constraints for the relationships between all the geometric entity data types specified in ISO 10303-42, the STEP geometry/topology resource [19]. However, the newly developed STEP resource ISO 10303-108 [5,9] focuses on a smaller selection of widely implemented geometric constraints, and provides 'freeform' constraint capabilities that can be used for more specialized cases.

There has been some discussion regarding whether geometric constraints should best be specified between geometric or topological elements in a model [18,20]. ISO 10303-108 specifies such constraints exclusively between geometric elements. The representation, transfer

---

[1] IGES: Initial Graphics Exchange Specification; DXF: Autocad's Drawing eXchange Format; SAT: Save ACIS Text.

and reconstruction of geometric elements selected from the screen display by the CAD system user as constraint elements (or for other purposes) is a crucial aspect of the exchange of procedural or construction history models.

The work described in the present paper is aimed at preserving, as far as is possible, all aspects of design intent including relationships implied by the constructional operations used. The approach described by Rappoport [13], based on the concept of 'feature rewrites,' appears to concentrate more on consistency of pure geometry between the original and the received models. One example given by Rappoport concerns the replacement of an extrusion feature created by extruding up to a specified surface by an extrusion having a specified length, with an identical geometric result. This may be satisfactory from the geometric point of view, but it loses the 'design intent' characteristic that was present in the original system, where modification of the specified surface will automatically lead to a consistent modification of the extrusion.

Another approach to the exchange of procedural models, demonstrated at KAIST (Korea Advanced Institute of Science and Technology) in Korea, is based on the capture and transfer of the journal file created by CAD systems, which contains a record of every action of the system user [21,22]. In the past this has used a STEP-like neutral format for the representation of a common command set. The work of the KAIST team is now migrating towards a strict ISO 10303 methodology. They have developed a new resource — ISO 10303-112 — that provides for the exchange of procedural representations of 2D sketches. It will make use of the ISO 10303-55 mechanisms for the representation of construction history and ISO 10303-108 for the representation of parameters and constraints. Previous ISO 10303 parametric exchanges have relied on the direct importation of explicitly defined sketches into the construction history. Another difference with the previous ISO 10303 approach to parametric models is that ISO 10303-112 does not require the transfer of an explicit 'current result' model with the construction history of a sketch.

Ideally, in a standard for the exchange of procedurally represented CAD models, the set of modeling operations defined should be the union of the operation sets of all CAD systems. However, this would give rise to a very large and complex standard that would require constant updating. The present approach is to try to define the set of common capabilities of the operation sets of the most widely used commercially available CAD systems, and to base the standard on that. Inevitably, some CAD systems will have capabilities that lie outside this range. Thus complete information exchange, if possible at all, will require the representation of any such capability in terms of lower-level capabilities in the common set, with some probable loss of semantic information.

ISO 10303-111 ('Elements for the procedural representation of solid shapes'), which was recently published by ISO [7,23], provides representations of operations for the construction of feature-based solid models. A construction history capability is under development for Edition 2 of ISO 10303-203, the initial version is the most widely used STEP application protocol.

A report on the recently completed PDES Inc. project CHAPS ('Construction History And ParametricS') [12] provides a business case for the transfer of construction history models with and without parameterization and constraints. Little technical detail is given. CHAPS used development versions of ISO 10303-55, -108 and --111, and the emphasis was on the transfer of procedural (construction history) models defined solely by feature operations, in which parameters and constraints are for the most part implicit. The project described in the present paper focuses more on the transfer of procedural models containing explicitly defined parameters and constraints, and we provide more technical detail of problem classification and solution. The exchange of procedural models without explicit parameters or constraints, as in the first phase of the CHAPS project, gives some level of editability in the receiving system but omits certain aspects of design intent information that may be crucial in maintaining product functionality after a modification.

As mentioned above, two new STEP resources, ISO 10303-55 and -108, have been published earlier, and a third ISO 10303-111 has been published recently (early 2007). These provide the basic resources needed for the exchange of construction history CAD models with parameterization and constraints, and allow the capture and transfer of much of the design intent information present in the sending system. ISO 10303-109, also recently published, provides representations for the exchange of feature-based assembly models with parameters and constraints used to defined kinematic relationships, but this paper does not address the exchange of assembly data.

ISO 10303-108 defines standardized neutral representations for the exchange of the following fundamental concepts associated with parametric models [24]:

- parameters (including dimensional parameters), in particular the ability to associate a parameter with an attribute of an entity instance.
- explicit constraints, covering the three types of constraints defined in more detail later: algebraic, logical, and dimensional. (In the second and third cases definitions are provided for the majority of widely used geometric constraints, in a descriptive manner, allowing sending and receiving systems to formulate them mathematically in whatever way is convenient for their internal functionality.)
- sketches, specialized 2D constructs that may incorporate parameterization and constraints. (Sketch elements may be constrained with respect to each other, or with respect to elements lying outside the sketch.)

Our approach is an advance over the previous work reviewed above in several respects:

1. *Use of a dual model for exchange of parametric construction history models.* The primary procedural model defines the construction history. It has an associated secondary model of the B-rep or some closely related explicit type. The secondary model can be used in the receiving system to check the validity of the model transfer. This can be done by comparing the reconstructed explicit model in that system, generated by evaluating the transferred primary model, with the transferred secondary model. The secondary model can also be used to resolve ambiguities, e.g., to determine which of several valid solutions of a nonlinear constraint system was chosen by the designer using the originating system.

2. *The transfer of parameters and mathematical relations between parameters.* In principle, any numerical attribute in the part model can be treated as a parameter in an exchange. This makes it possible, for example, to transfer a relation defining the number of hole instances in a circular hole pattern in terms of the radius of the pattern.

3. *Ability to handle several types of constraints (algebraic, logical, dimensional) in a very general and easily extensible manner.*

4. *Preservation of multiple simultaneous parameter relationships in the model rather than a set of independent relationships.* Previous work has been less general in this respect [13, 22].

5. *Conformity to the international standard ISO 10303 by using newly published parts of that standard·*

3. INFORMATION CLASSIFICATION FOR STEP-BASED TRANSLATION OF PARAMETRIC MODELS

This section discusses the classification of information concerning parameters, constraints and geometry. Such a classification is important because different use cases require different algorithms to handle them. Section 5 will use the criteria given in this section to show how interoperability may be achieved for 19 cases of parameter usage, 7 cases of constraint usage and several distinct cases of geometry usage.

Some examples of STEP entities in partial STEP exchange files are given in this section and later in the paper. To understand these it is useful to know that entity types as defined in ISO 10303 are conventionally written in text in **bold_type** with underscores between the words forming the entity name. Exchange files contain instances of these entity types. Each instance has a numerical identifier, e.g., #1234, and the entity name (which appears in upper case in an exchange file) is followed by a list of values of the attributes of the entity for the particular instance concerned. Further details are given in section 6.2. It is also important to note that the work reported in this paper was carried out using development versions of the relevant ISO 10303 documents. Detail changes have been made to these documents in the meantime, but there has been no change in their basic principles.

3.1 Overview

ISO 10303-203 (AP203 of STEP) [14] does not support the exchange of features, parameters, constraints or construction history information, but only the final shape of a CAD model [2]. As far as shape is concerned, an AP203 model file therefore contains only geometrical and topological information relating to the final designed shape of the model. The transfer file contains no details of the construction history of the model. For example, if an edge is picked from a cubic block and a chamfer feature is created on it, the AP203 file will contain information about the chamfer face, but details of the original edge will have been lost. In the work reported here, any such B-rep elements existing at intermediate stages of the design but which are invisible or inactive in the final B-rep model are included in the transmitted parametric model. This is necessary because any such element may have been used as the reference element for a dimensional or other constraint, or as a reference for feature creation. Thus the present work captures important aspects of the construction history of a transferred model. It also transfers details of parameterization and explicit constraints as defined in the sending system, and therefore captures important aspects of design intent that are lost in AP203 transfers.

Dimensional information can, in principle, sometimes be inferred by examination of geometric relationships between geometric elements of a model in an AP203 exchange file. That

---

[2] This remark applies to Edition 1 of AP203. Edition 2, now in preparation, will contain construction history capabilities.

is a dangerous practice, because the model contains no intimation of the dimensioning scheme actually used by the designer. In any case, the elements related by dimensional relationships established early in the design process are often no longer present in the final version of the model, having been modified or deleted by subsequent modeling operations. In modern dimension driven parametric CAD systems the values of many dimensions are specified during the design process as inputs to the constructional procedures used in building the model. Such implicitly defined dimensions are not accessible to the CAD system's constraint solver/constraint manager, which provides the variational capabilities of the system. They can only be changed by re-running the construction history with modified input values. In the variational case, dimensions and constraints are accessible to the constraint manager, which solves the constraint system for values of the appropriate parameters, then sends their values to the geometry engine, which re-evaluates the B-rep model and displays it on the screen.

In the work described here, the model exchange covers:

- geometry: active or inactive, visible or invisible, selectable or un-selectable, intermediate B-rep entities and datums, of every geometric type defined in ISO 10303-42 [19], as discussed in what follows.
- design features (though strictly these are nothing more than high-level definitions of local geometric configurations, having no associated application semantics, that are captured during the design process).
- construction history.
- Parameterization.
- constraints: algebraic, logical and dimensional (see the definitions below).

Fig. 2 shows the information elements in a CAD model, together with the corresponding ISO 10303 integrated resource schemas and the parts of the overall standard in which they are defined. The diagram covers procedural models with parameterization and constraints, together with the secondary explicit model (usually of the B-rep type) used in dual model exchanges. The integrated resources shown in the table are assumed to be used by a hypothetical application protocol (AP) using (among other parts) ISO 10303-42, -55, -108 and -111, in the absence of any currently published AP with the required capabilities. As mentioned earlier, it is intended that a future edition of AP203 [23] will eventually include some or all of them.

Two important aims of this section are:
1. The clarification of the meaning of the terms used in Fig. 2, which are used in different and conflicting ways in various research projects and by different CAD system developers.
2. The selection and expression of the information that must be transmitted in a complete CAD model exchange (this is necessary because the interpretation of such terms differs widely between CAD systems).

For example, the meaning of the word 'parameter' has various interpretations in the documentation of different CAD systems, not all of them compatible with ISO 10303 usage. Additionally, many CAD systems do not recognize the existence of the implicit parameters arising in the use of feature-based creation operations, regarding them as having little in common with explicitly defined parameters directly created by the user.

Parameters Parameterization		Schema	Part 108		
Equations		Explicit constraint Schema			
Dimensions		Explicit geometric constraint schema		Part 42	B-Rep geometry and topology
Constraints					
Features	Sketch-based	Sketch schema			
	Fillet, Hole, etc.	Solid shape element schema	Part 111		
	Pattern				
Construction History		Procedural shape model schema	Part 55		
Parametric History-Based Model (1st model)				2nd (explicit) model	

Fig. 2. Scope of the Hypothetical Application Protocol

3.2 Parameters

3.2.1 Criteria for the classification of parameters

Often, the interpretation of technical terms in CAD system documentation is narrower and more restricted than is the case in ISO 10303 or an academic research environment. This is because every commercial system developer's horizon is limited by the specialized functionality and performance characteristics of the system concerned. Taking a broad interpretation, the term *parameter* may be considered to include a dimension of the part or one of its individual features, an item in a design table family, or some other numerical value such as a user-defined property value. A typical narrow interpretation of the term is taken in the CAD system Pro/Engineer®, where it is used exclusively for a value explicitly added to the model by the user. Some commercial CAD systems provide a unified data structure for all parameters, but others implement several specialized data structures for specific kinds of parameters used to represent *feature attributes or properties，variables，dimensions，parameters，* some of these terms having slightly different interpretations in the different systems. For example a numerical value that may be changed is often displayed to the designer as a dimension and is handled internally in a data structure restricted to the representation of dimensions, e.g., ProDimension in Pro/Engineer®, IDisplayDimension in Solidworks®. Successful ISO 10303 exchange of parametric models, therefore, requires all relevant parameters (in a general sense) to be extracted from a variety of diverse data structures in the various CAD systems, with no omissions. The criteria used in this paper for distinguishing different parameter types are given in Table 1. Such distinctions are necessary because the different cases require different algorithms to handle them, and it is necessary to avoid the creation of spurious parameters during the transfer. It should be mentioned here that ISO 10303-108 defines a unified general representation for explicit parameters with real, integer, boolean or string values, whose precise application is intended to be apparent from the context in which they are used.

Table 1. Criteria for parameter classification

Criterion #	Distinction
Criterion 0	numeric vs. non-numeric
Criterion 1	bound vs. unbound
Criterion 2	dimensional vs. non-dimensional
Criterion 3	explicit vs. implicit
Criterion 4	dependent, independent, or free

- *Criterion 0* (numeric vs. non-numeric): The dimensional characteristics of a feature can be given explicitly as numerical values, but other properties can be specified non-numerically. For example, a cylindrical hole feature may be provided with an enumerated choice of flat, hemispherical or conical bottom surface.

- *Criterion 1* (bound vs. unbound): this distinction is made in ISO 10303-108. A bound parameter is one which is associated with (or *bound to*) an attribute of some instance in the exchange file, whose value is potentially variable following the exchange. An unbound parameter is not directly associated with an attribute in that manner, but participates in a specified mathematical relationship that may control the values of one or more bound parameters.

- *Criterion 2* (dimensional vs. non-dimensional): A dimensional parameter, which represents a dimension explicitly, is created when the designer uses a 'dimension command' as provided by the CAD system user interface. Explicit dimensions are usually associated with sketch construction, whereas feature creation operations usually give rise to implicit dimensions (see below). CAD systems in general distinguish between dimensional parameters, which they refer to simply as *dimensions*, and non-dimensional parameters, which they refer to as *parameters*. An example of a non-dimensional parameter is the number of holes in a circular pattern of holes. ISO 10303-108 treats both types of parameters in a unified way; in this context, a dimensional parameter is usually one whose value is of type **length_measure** or **plane_angle_measure.**

- *Criterion 3* (implicit vs. explicit): In either the dimensional or non-dimensional case, an explicit parameter is created when the designer uses a command for its creation, whereas an implicit parameter is automatically created as a (potentially variable) attribute of a created feature. Some CAD systems create distinct data structures for recording and handling implicit and explicit dimensions.

- *Criterion 4* (dependent, independent, free): a dependent parameter is one whose value is governed by a constraint and can only be changed by modification of independent elements in that constraint. An independent parameter is one whose value is editable and can be used to govern the values of other elements in a constraint. A free parameter is one that is associated with some attribute of the model but is not involved in any constraint.

3.2.2 Explicit parameters

With regard to Criterion 3 above, experience in developing the proof-of-concept translators has shown the virtues of writing explicit parameters into the neutral exchange file whenever possible. This allows the maximal preservation of an important aspect of design intent. In the ISO 10303 context, an explicit parameter is any subtype of the ISO 10303-108 **variational_parameter** entity. Most CAD systems support the explicit parameter functionality, for the following purposes:

- o specification of important geometric or non-geometric properties of the part
- o association of a user-defined name with an attribute or implicit parameter in the model
- o making an implicit parameter visible to the user
- o specification of additional information for a feature attribute
- o reduction of the number of degrees of freedom of the transmitted model
- o definition of constraint relations based on mathematical relationships

ISO 10303-108 makes provision for these requirements as follows:

1. *Specification of important geometric or non-geometric properties of the part:* This is necessary in geometric situations that are not covered by the range of feature creation operations provided. In this case instances of the ISO 10303-108 entity **variational_parameter** must be associated with dimensional or other attributes in the model and used to control values or relationships as appropriate.

2. *Making an implicit parameter visible to the user of the receiving system:* This is simply done by associating an instance of **variational_parameter** with the model attribute that represents the implicit parameter;

3. *Association of a user-defined name with an attribute or implicit parameter in the model* : Again, an instance of **variational_parameter** is associated with the attribute or implicit parameter, and its name attribute used to specify the desired user-defined name.

4. *Specification of additional information for a feature attribute* : For example, ISO 10303-108 provides for the association of a valid domain of values for any instance of **variational_parameter**. For numerical parameters, the domain may be a continuous interval or a discrete set of values. Such domains can only be specified for explicitly defined parameters. Implicit parameters are normally restricted only as to the type of their values. Domain specification is achieved by association of an explicit parameter with the attribute corresponding to the implicit parameter, as for the previous two cases, and setting its domain attribute as desired.

5. *Reduction of the number of degrees of freedom of the transmitted model* : This application is closely related to the previous one. All quantities defined in the sending system should be regarded as potentially variable, unless they are specifically constrained to be constant. If values of dimensional or other attributes are fixed in the sending system, this fact can be captured in the exchange file through the use of the ISO 10303-108 entity **fixed_instance_attribute_set**, which would make their invariance clear to the receiving system. Effectively, this is equivalent to associating an explicit parameter with each of the attributes concerned and restricting its domain to a single value.

6. *Definition of constraint relations based on mathematical relationships* : ISO 10303-108 provides for the representation of mathematical relationships between instances of **variational_parameter**. Some of those instances may be associated with dimensional attributes in the model. The use of ISO 10303-108 entity **free_form_assignment** or

free_form_relationship constraints allows the specification of mathematical dependencies between the values of those attributes.

Many CAD systems create a 'Part Family' table that allows the user convenient access to details of independent explicit parameters in a model and any relations defined between them. If the domain of a parameter is a set of discrete values, then those values can be specified in the table. Any type of independent value may be included in a table, but dependent variables are not generally included because their values can be derived from the relations that define them. Thus the table contains a set of independent sketch parameters defining all admissible members of the part family defined by the parametric model. A single CAD model may have several such alternative configurations associated with it, one of which will represent the 'current result', i.e., the set of parameters used to generate the current model as displayed on the screen of the sending system. Since the relevant information is available in the table, any value occurring there in the sending system can be represented as an instance of ISO 10303-108 **variational_parameter** in an exchange file. Correspondingly, parameter information transmitted in an ISO 10303 exchange file can be used by the receiving system to construct a part family table in the receiving system; it is simply a matter of organizing the information appropriately. However, it should be noted that conditional parameter relationships of the IF – THEN – ELSE type, which can be defined in the part family tables of some CAD systems, are not yet available in ISO 10303.

3.3 Constraints

Constraints specify relationships between elements of a model that are required to be maintained if the model is edited. Bettig & Shah [18] distinguish the following types of geometric constraints:

- o *algebraic*, in which a mathematical relationship is required to hold between two or more parameters of the model.
- o *logical*, in which a specified geometric relationship between geometric elements is required to be true.
- o *dimensional*, in which a distance or angle relationship is specified between geometrical entities (possibly subject to some permitted range of variation when the model is edited).

In ISO 10303-108, most dimensional constraints are specified as subtypes of logical constraints. Thus, for example, an instance of **parallel_geometric_constraint** is a logical assertion that members of a set of lines or planes are parallel to each other, while an instance of **pgc_with_dimension** ('parallel geometric constraint with dimension') asserts that the distance between precisely two parallel elements has a specified value.

Sketch constraints are different in some respects from other types of constraints. Specifically, they define relationships between 2D sketch elements, and they may be stored by CAD systems in a specialized constraint data structure. Other uses of constraints, including the specification of inter-feature relationships and inter-part relationships in an assembly, are defined in 3D. In the inter-feature case they usually reference datums or other auxiliary geometric elements rather than elements of the current state of the actual part geometry. There is some variation between systems in the way 3D constraints are handled, but as noted in Restriction 2 specified below, the implementation described in the present paper deals only with constraints defined in the sketch context.

Explicit constraints are represented as individual entities in the model, specifying particular relationships between two or more of its elements. Constraints of this type are created deliberately by the user, who might constrain (for example) a line to be horizontal, or two lines to be parallel, or two parameters to satisfy a specified mathematical relationship.

By contrast, an implicit constraint has no representation as an entity in the model, but occurs automatically due to the action of a constructional procedure [5,25]. During sketch creation, different CAD systems will give rise to different combinations of implicit and explicit constraints, depending, for example, on whether the system handles only fully constrained sketches or whether it allows partially constrained situations. If under-constrained situations are not allowed, the system will automatically create implicit constraints to remove any remaining degrees of freedom. Conversely, if under-constrained sketches are allowed, the designer may at some later design stage finalize the sketch by adding explicit constraints to resolve any remaining ambiguity. In the exchange of sketch information it is fortunate that even constraints created automatically by the system are usually given explicit representations in the system database. An operation to create a fillet arc to round the junction between two line segments, for example, generally gives rise to the explicit representation of two tangency constraints referring to the arc and the two lines concerned. In some systems it is possible to turn off the automatic generation of these design intent relations. This should not be done if it may be required to transmit the model concerned to some other system, because crucial information will then be lost.

Several restrictions apply to the types of constraints handled in the implementation reported here:

1. Implicit sketch constraints have not been considered. If a sketch constraint is not explicitly represented in the CAD model in the sending system, it would be necessary to use constraint recognition to detect its presence, and experience has shown that this is a dangerous process. Intended constraints may be missed, but more importantly unintended 'constraints' may be recognized from chance geometric relationships [26]. If the CAD system allows under-constrained sketches then constraint recognition is not necessary, as mentioned above. If the system permits only fully-constrained sketches, we have assumed that every constraint, including all those created automatically by the system, will be represented explicitly in the model.
2. In the implementation described here, the only explicit constraints considered are those defined in the context of a 2D sketch. The only 3D constraints that are captured and transmitted are those that are inherent in feature definitions. Where datums are defined, they are transmitted in the neutral file as auxiliary geometry. Details will be given in the next section.
3. The range of constraints considered is limited to those defined in ISO 10303-108. That document includes all the most widely implemented geometric constraints, and additionally provides a general mechanism that can be used to achieve the effects of more specialized constraints when necessary [24].
4. As previously mentioned, ISO 10303 currently provides no mechanism for defining conditional mathematical relationships between parameters based on structures of the IF – THEN – ELSE type. These may be provided in the future, but in the meantime such constructs are out of scope in the present implementation.

5. The work reported is confined to the exchange of single part models; assemblies have been left for the future.

3.4 Geometry

This section discusses the representation of geometry in CAD systems, and examines some associated translation issues. A classification of geometric information is proposed for distinguishing the different classes of geometric information transmitted in an ISO 10303 exchange. If a commercial CAD system does not provide adequate API (Application Programming Interface) functionality for accessing its internal database, alternative ways must be sought for acquiring necessary geometric information.

3.4.1 Types of geometry in a CAD model

A CAD system database contains details of the geometry of all features in the model as initially created. In some systems, if a subsequent modification changes the topology of an existing feature, the geometry of the modified feature is also recorded. If a feature is suppressed (as not being necessary for some desired application) or the geometry is not relevant in the current configuration of the model, the database records the suppressed or invisible geometry. However, as it is not displayed on the CAD system screen it is not selectable by the user for modification of the model. Any created dimension, constraint or feature makes reference to one or more existing geometric elements of the model, or auxiliary elements acting as datums. This reference geometry must be visible and selectable at the time when it is referenced, though it may not be visible in the final model at the time of translation, having been suppressed or overwritten by that time. The transmission of procedural or construction history models therefore requires the exchange medium to be able to reference previously selectable elements that are not selectable in the current result at the time of transfer. ISO 10303-55 supports the exchange of explicit elements for this purpose in such a way that the corresponding element of the explicit model under reconstruction in the receiving system can be identified and used appropriately as a reference element or datum in the reconstruction process.

3.4.2 Classification of geometry in parametric data exchange

The role of the program that writes the exchange file is to capture the maximum of information from the model in the sending system that will contribute towards its successful reconstruction in the receiving system. Essentially, this covers:

- elements participating in the final B-rep model
- elements created during the construction procedure of the final B-rep model
- elements not present in the final model but which are used as reference elements for dimensions or constraints
- elements of sketches used as input by construction procedures

In what follows, geometric and topological entities will be denoted by G, while B_n will denote the nth model in the succession of 'current result' B-rep models generated by the system at the various stages of the design. In Fig. 3, the model B_1 is the result of extruding an L-shaped sketch, B_2 shows the result of adding a hole feature and B_3 the result of rounding one of the edges of B_2.

19

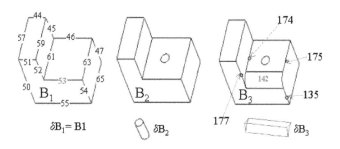

Fig.3. Example of geometry identification (L-block model)

In the translator implementation described later, geometric and topological elements are classified in the following manner. Each feature creation operation gives rise to certain elements associated with that feature. The only elements in the model which do not belong to features are auxiliary geometric items such as construction geometry or datums. The set of geometric or topological elements associated with the nth feature takes into account all differences between the nth secondary B-rep model and the ($n-1$)th such model, including pre-existing elements that were modified by the latest modeling operation. If we denote the set of all B-rep geometric entities in the CAD database at stage n by B_n, and the status at stage ($n-1$) by B_{n-1} then we can define the difference as $\delta B_n = B_n - B_{n-1}$. In the example shown in Fig. 3, model B_1 has 8 visible faces and 18 visible edges (visible in the sense that they can be seen in some orientation of the model), and no invisible entities. One of the edges of B_1 is rounded at a later stage, and that edge has become invisible in model B_3.

The geometrical and topological elements associated with a single feature creation operation can be divided into four classes for translation purposes:

o   *Class 1 geometry*: This includes all geometric elements generated by one feature creation operation. In Fig. 3, the Class 1 geometry of B_3 includes not only face 142, which was created as a result of the rounding, but all the geometric and topological elements defining delta volume δB_2 together with all the elements such as faces 135, 174, 175 and 177 which previously existed but were modified by the creation of the rounded edge. Edge 53 is needed as a reference for the creation of the rounding in the receiving system, but it is not included in the Class 1 geometry at this stage.

o   *Class 2 geometry* : This class contains elements that are selected by the user from the system screen as the basis for feature operations. An example is Edge 53 that is selected at the second stage in Fig. 3 as the basis for the rounding operation whose result is evident in the third stage. All CAD systems provide the means for identification, in the system database, of specific topological elements selected in this way. In the example given, it is clear that Edge 53 is not part of the stage 3 B-rep. It is nevertheless necessary to represent it in the procedural model to indicate unambiguously which edge was rounded.

o   *Class 3 geometry* : This class consists of sketch elements. Sketches are explicitly modeled 2D shape constructs that are normally represented and managed by CAD systems separately from the 3D B-rep models in whose construction history they participate. For example, if a planar face in a B-rep model is used as the basis for a sketch and further operations then modify or delete that face, the sketch it was used to

define will persist unmodified in the system database. Many dimensions and constraints applying to 3D B-rep models are originally created in 2D sketches.

- o *Class 4 geometry*: This class contains elements that are not part of the feature geometry but are used as reference elements for constraining or positioning a feature, or for similar purposes in the plane of a sketch. All datums in CAD models are stored as explicit elements that are compatible with designer's view of the datum but may differ in detail aspects. For example, a system may use an unbounded line as a datum, but displays it on the system screen as a bounded line segment.

All four classes of geometry must be transferred to enable the correct reconstruction of each feature in the receiving system. The translator implementation reported here compiles, for each feature, a list of geometric instances belonging to each class.

Examples: Edges 52, 54, 61, and 63 are not elements of the Class 1 geometry for the third stage shown in Fig. 3 because they do not exist in their original forms at that stage. At the third stage, Face 142 and its edges are clearly Class 1 elements of the rounding feature, because they were created by the associated feature operation. The same applies to Edges 135, 174, 175 and 177, which are modifications of the four first stage edges listed earlier.

4. INFORMATION STRUCTURING FOR STEP-BASED PARAMETRIC TRANSLATION

In this section the 'ownership' of dimensions, constraints and parameters is defined, and a hierarchical information structure is presented. The structuring of information is important, because it enables the definition of 'units of creation'. The translation process can then be expressed in terms of mappings of units of creation from the sending system to the STEP exchange file and from that file to the receiving system. The entire translation process then becomes a sequence of such mappings. This approach simplifies both the conception and the implementation of translators. The defined structure is used for checking interoperability (as described in section 5), and for creating the prototype translator (as described in section 6).

4.1 The ownership and structuring of identifiers

Most CAD systems maintain the sequence of operations used to create a part in a design feature tree, which is similar to a constructive solid geometry (CSG) tree. In parametric or feature-based data exchange, a given feature-based parametric history graph in a source system is mapped to a corresponding graph in the target system that generates similar (ideally, identical) geometry while preserving as much design intent information as possible [27].

The information written into the exchange file is derived from the model file stored in the originating CAD system via the system's applications programming interface (API). It does not correspond to the complete history of the operations used by the designer, because that may contain (for example) errors, error recovery operations, trial modifications aimed at finding an optimal configuration, and graphical commands that do not change the model but only its appearance on the screen. The model file is re-evaluated after every creation or modification operation. It therefore represents a cleaned up history with all extraneous operations omitted.

The goal in the work described here is the automatic identification what may be called 'units of construction' that have the same number of degrees of freedom in both the CAD system and the ISO 10303 neutral file. Depending on the nature of the system and the granularity of its representation, this may require the matching of a set of finer granularity system creation operations to a single ISO 10303 operation of coarser granularity, or vice versa. A one-to-one mapping would be ideal, of course, as shown in the 'direct' case of Fig. 4 below, but differences between CAD systems are such that this is possible only in rare cases.

Figure 4 shows the four possibilities for identifying units of construction. These should be regarded as applying to either of the two translation stages: (i) writing from the sending system to the ISO 10303 file or (ii) reading from the ISO 10303 file to the receiving system. The *aggregation* case combines lower-level elements into higher-level groups for transfer, while the *decomposition* case splits high-level elements into lower-level ones. Inevitably, in many cases some complex combination of these two approaches will need to be used. This emphasizes the virtues of transmitting the model in feature-based units smaller than the entire part model, because the number of possibilities for many-to-many mappings at the model level would be unsupportable for complex models made up of many thousands of elements.

Mapping links disappear in many cases, and for different reasons. Some examples follow:

o Features defined in CAD systems may have no direct correspondences in ISO 10303-111. For example, in some systems features include the datum points, lines and planes used for dimensioning or as reference elements in constraints. Such elements are therefore stored in feature data structures, whereas in ISO 10303 they come under the heading of "auxiliary geometric elements" as defined in ISO 10303-108. Thus an element that the sending system regards as a feature must often be written into the exchange file as a simple geometric element.

o The creation of a simple constant radius blend feature will usually lead to the designer's chosen blend radius being stored by the system as an attribute of the feature representation, possibly with some default value, and not as an explicit dimension. However, the radius information is accessible to the ISO 10303 translator, and a corresponding explicit dimension can be created in the receiving system if that is appropriate.

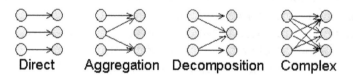

Direct   Aggregation   Decomposition   Complex

Fig. 4. Mapping classes

Every integer sequence number in an ISO 10303 exchange file is the unique identifier of a transferred entity instance. The entity types concerned include feature construction operations, geometric and topological elements, mathematical relationships, and explicit parameters, constraints and dimensions.   CAD systems use different schemes for assigning internal identifiers to model elements. In some systems, for example Pro/Engineer®, each feature, topological element and geometric element has an integer identifier that is unique in the model. However, in most feature-based CAD systems, this is not the case, because the information is structured around feature entities and identifiers are only unique within a feature. Similarly, a sketch segment identifier may be unique in the model or unique only in the sketch, though the latter case is more usual.

CAD system APIs provide the translator developer with a 'model pointer' that can be used as the initial point of the implementation. It provides access to various lists of entities occurring in the referenced model. In many cases, there are functional dependencies in CAD system data structures. For example, each feature generally has associated constraints and associated dimensions. These can be accessed first by getting the list of feature pointers from the 'model pointer', and then following them to access the list of constraints or dimensions belonging to each feature.

In the case of a sketch-based feature, sketch creation is treated as a single operation — a sketch may contain many elements, but its parametric variation is determined not by a replay of its construction history but by computation of a new solution to its constraint system.

Most CAD systems do not allow the definition of explicit constraints between elements of more than one sketch. Each sketch constraint is therefore usually unique to one sketch, and a functional dependency exists between the constraint and the sketch. A constraint between sketch elements is only indirectly accessible by the model through reference to the sketch concerned, which may be considered to be a separate submodel in its own right [17]. However, sketch elements may also be constrained with respect to datums or other geometric elements that are defined outside the sketch context and are more directly accessible.

To provide maximum compatibility with a wide range of CAD modeling methodologies, schemas in the ISO 10303 resource parts define entities at a very general level. In particular, there are no specialized links between the sketch and feature entities of ISO 10303-111 and the dimensional or other constraint entities defined in ISO 10303-108. The translation processors therefore need to identify the sketch or feature relationships for each constraint indirectly by comparing the geometric elements involved in that constraint with elements of sketch or feature geometry. For example, if the type and attributes of a geometric element involved in a constraint match (to within the system tolerance) with an element of a **positioned_sketch** instance in the model, then we can infer that the constraint was associated with that sketch in the originating system. The most robust exchanges will be those in which all constraints can be assigned to sketches or features in this way.

The basic principle of the exchange of feature-based construction history CAD models is that each successive feature creation operation is mapped onto a corresponding operation or sequence of operations in the receiving system. This allows us to decompose the overall process into simpler components, and to optimize the transfer of individual features. Then, ideally, following the same sequence for the mapped operations in the receiving system will result in a correct reconstruction there. It is a characteristic of this process that the partial models generated at various stages of the overall reconstruction process will also match the corresponding partial models created during the original design process.

4.2 Level of feature data exchange

There are several ways of representing and exchanging features. In this paper, we recognize three levels of feature data exchange, Levels 1 and 3 being opposite extreme cases and Level 2 the general case. Level 1 is the simplest approach, but it is unfortunately inadequate for the representation and exchange of real engineering shapes.

4.2.1 Level 1: Translation at the level of features as provided in the CAD system user interface (*coarse granularity*).

If the feature as it occurs in the sending system is exactly compatible with a construct defined in the ISO 10303 integrated resources (in particular, ISO 10303-42 for swept solids and boolean combinations and ISO 10303-111 for more general features), the STEP construct can be used directly. In this case, the number of implicit parameters in the CAD system is exactly same as the number of attributes of the STEP feature entity. In general, constraints are implicit in this case, as in the case of the parallelism and perpendicularity constraints applying to the faces of the **block** entity defined in Part 42. The exception is the use of explicit constraints on elements of a sketch profile to be extruded, as in the case of the **extruded_face_solid_with_trim_conditions** defined in Part 111.

In the case of a block feature, the attributes of the **block** entity in Part 42 of STEP are a position and orientation attribute of type **axis2_placement_3d** plus three dimensional attributes named **x,y,z,** of type **positive_length_measure**. In the simplest case, the block can be transmitted as an element of a Part 55 **procedural_solid_representation_sequence**. Then, the dimensions of the block arise as values of the attributes of the block instance in the operation sequence. Editability in the receiving system is achieved by re-running the operation sequence with changed values of those attributes. How the receiving system represents the dimensional attributes is no concern of Part 108 — the necessary information is present in the file, and can be rewritten in any way that is appropriate to that system's internal functionality. In this simplest case, the fact that **x,y** and **z** are of type **positive_length_measure** implies that their values lie in the open interval $(0,\infty)$.

In the case of an extrusion, the ISO 10303-42 entity **extruded_face_solid** may be used, unless the extrusion has specialized end conditions, when the subtype **extruded_face_solid_with_trim_conditions** (EFSWTC), as defined in ISO 10303-111, is appropriate. The sketch used for the cross-section of the extrusion can be represented as an instance of **face_surface.** Any constraints applying to the sketch can added as relationships between the point and curve elements composing the boundary of the **face_surface.** If any aspect of the feature cannot be captured as the value of an attribute of the EFSWTC creation operation then it is necessary to resort to one of the lower granularity approaches described below.

4.2.2 Level 2: Translation using a combination of approximately compatible feature representations and lower level entities (*intermediate granularity*).

In many cases, CAD system features do not map one-to-one onto ISO 10303-42 or -111 features, because the latter represent a compromise intended to give approximate compatibility with a wide range of CAD systems. For example, in the creation of a rectangular protrusion feature, some systems (but not all) allow the boolean union of a block primitive feature with the part volume. In a system that does not provide a block primitive, a corresponding block may be constructed as a **swept_face_solid** based on a 2D rectangular sketch with parallelism, perpendicularity and dimensional constraints applied to its sides. In case of the L-block of Fig. 3 it is not necessary to specify an explicit dimension for the extrusion distance, because that is represented as the value of an attribute of the entity instance representing the creation of the extrusion. However, geometric constructions that do not conform to any of the standard feature configurations provided by ISO 10303-42 or -111 must generally be built in terms of lower-level elements that may include explicit dimensions or constraints.

For a successful mapping between different granularities of representation, the number of degrees of freedom on both sides of the mapping should be the same. On either side, some of those degrees of freedom may be expressed in terms of explicit parameters, others implicitly as values of attributes in a construction operation. If the combination of explicit and implicit parameters is different on the two sides of the mapping some information structuring will be necessary, as described below.

While some CAD systems provide more than one hundred variations on the hole creation operation, ISO 10303-111 provides a much smaller set of possibilities. Thus, in mapping a hole feature from the sending system into an ISO 10303 exchange file, the ISO 10303-111 feature that provides the closest match should first be selected. Any additional characteristics of the sending system feature that have not been captured can then be mapped using lower-level elements such as ISO 10303-108 constraints.

Consider the example of a simple cylindrical blind hole with a flat bottom. In CAD system **A,** the operation for creating such a hole may require four parameters, two to position it in the plane of a face, plus a radius and a depth. In CAD system **B**, the creation operation may only require the radius and depth parameters, while the positioning of the hole is a separate operation requiring values for the two further parameters. The simplest case of the ISO 10303-111 round hole feature requires values for radius and depth attributes plus a reference to an **axis2_placement_3d** that defines the hole axis and positions the feature in the model; it therefore matches the methodology of system **A**. If such a hole definition is transferred into system **B** the program that reads the exchange file will need to break it down into the definition of a 2-parameter hole creation operation plus a positioning operation. In this example the granularity of System A is coarser than that of system **B**.

Geometric elements of supporting instances, such as the **axis2_placement_3d** instance referred to above, are extracted from the sending system and transmitted as explicit elements in the exchange file. In the case of datum geometry, different CAD systems use internal representations with different levels of detail. As much detail as possible needs to be extracted from the sending system for transmission, to allow the receiving system flexibility in the reconstruction of datums.

Parameters should be preserved whenever possible; if for some reason a parameter is not accessible through the API of the sending system its details should be inferred as far as possible from other contextual data.

4.2.3 Level 3: Translation in terms of low-level geometry and topology from Part 42 (*fine granularity*)

The block primitive referred to above may in principle be exchanged as a complete B-rep model, with parallelism, perpendicularity and distance constraints applied to the planes of its six faces, twelve edges and eight vertices. In this case, only Part 42 low-level geometrical and topological elements will be used, together with explicit constraints from Part 108. This approach is unlikely to be used for the transfer of commonly defined primitive shapes or features in a real situation, though it is useful for illustrative purposes and may have applications in the exchange of specialized user-defined features.

4.2.4 Summary

Translation should be performed at the feature level whenever possible, as this preserves the highest level of user intent. Account must be taken of whether the sending system allows only fully-constrained features or whether it permits under-constrained features. If a fully-constrained feature strategy is used, all intra-feature constraints are built into the definition of the feature and are therefore implicit, with the exception of any explicit constraints occurring in 2D sketches used in the feature definition. Often, feature definitions in ISO 10303-111 have a more general specification than the corresponding CAD system features, and this allows the possibility of mapping the feature plus several additional constraints from the sending system to a single feature in the exchange file. This maximizes flexibility for interpretation of that feature in the receiving system. In reading from the exchange file, it is therefore important to select the most highly constrained compatible option from the feature library of the receiving system when the feature being transmitted has implicit constraints that cannot be changed after creation. Any remaining differences in the representation can then be taken into account using additional lower-level elements.

5. INFORMATION INTEROPERABILITY FOR ISO 10303-BASED PARAMETRIC TRANSLATION

In this section interoperability of parameters, constraints and selected geometric elements is discussed. Our aim is the preservation of information from the sending system through the neutral file to the receiving system, despite possible major differences in the way that information is represented in these three locations.

5.1 Overview and assumptions for interoperability

The most important difference between a CAD system data structure and a neutral data structure such as that provided by STEP is that the former is designed for efficiency and the latter for informational completeness. We must therefore expect them to differ significantly, but the hope is that effective mappings between the two can be found. The following assumptions are made in our approach:

1. Any design intent information that cannot be extracted from the model in the sending system via the system API cannot be transmitted. This implies, in particular, that the work carried out does not involve general mechanisms for the automated recognition of features or other implicitly defined model characteristics from the pure construction history. For example, the CAD system Solidworks® provides a capability for the creation of an arc in a sketch that is tangent to two other geometric elements at its end points. On the system screen the appropriate tangencies appear to be present, but no

explicitly represented tangency constraints are generated in the model. Such constraints therefore cannot be written into the exchange file, and they may be violated if the model is edited following the exchange.

2. ISO 10303-108 does not consider details of the behavior of the receiving system if the transmitted model is modified there. It only assumes that it is as far as possible intuitive for the system user. The work reported here makes the same assumption.

3. In variational CAD design, a parametric model may fail to regenerate correctly following a modification, raising the question of what parameter values lead to valid models [28]. This work does not address that issue; for a given parametric solid and its constraint schema, the only restrictions of parameter domains taken into account are those explicitly specified by the designer.

4. This work does not address explicit 3D constraints between part features, though that is necessary for complete exchange of design intent and will be provided in future developments.

5. If the API of a particular CAD system does not support a specific necessary functionality, then we cannot exchange complete design intent. For example, at least one widely used CAD system does not allow access to constraint information in the model [12].

6. Only the exchange of solid models is addressed, with focus on feature-based models constructed using the capabilities of ISO 10303-111.

7. The minimal criteria for a 'successful' parametric model exchange are the correct transmission of parameters and constraints and their appropriate interpretation in the receiving system.

5.2 Parameter Interoperability

Parts 55 and Part 108 together allow the transfer of hybrid model representations in which some types of information are represented explicitly and others implicitly. A parameter is a variable associated with some quantity in a model, used to control its dimensions or other gross characteristics. It may be thought of as an input to a procedure, in this case a procedure that computes one instance of a family of shape models [6]. There are three basic ways of creating a rectangular block solid, one corresponding to each of the three levels of granularity defined above, but none of them requires the presence of explicit parameters in the model, unless it is desired to specify one or more relationships controlling its defining dimensions.

Some CAD systems give access to lists of parameters directly through the graphical user interface (GUI), e.g., via the 'Expression' functionality of the Unigraphics® system. However, in many cases parameters may be scattered implicitly in the model representation, as attributes in diverse data structures concerned with dimensions, features, mathematical relations, etc.

Several CAD systems have two or more data structures for dimensions, distinguishing between user created explicit dimensions and automatically created implicit dimensions. In such systems (for example, Pro/Engineer® and Solidworks®), implicit dimensions also have the effect of parameters. Implicitly defined parameters may be invisible from the GUI and only be accessible via the system API. For example, if the designer creates a fillet but does not specify a radius for it, a default value is assigned to that radius. That default value is not regarded as a dimension in the same sense as an explicitly created dimension. It is possible to change its value globally, and if that is done the radii of all fillets in the model will change. However the radius value is represented in the system, the important thing is that it exists, whether the user can see it through the GUI or not. If the system knows the value, it can be extracted and written into the exchange file.

Parameters are classified as shown in Table 2, which covers all possible cases. The table has 5 primary columns and three secondary columns Their significance is explained below. The primary columns relate to the criteria defined earlier, in Table 1 of Section 3.2.1.

The entity **variational_parameter** as defined in ISO 10303-108 can take values that are of types real, integer, boolean or string. An instance of such a parameter may be associated with a specified attribute of any entity instance in an exchange file, provided it has one of those types. Real-valued parameters are often associated with dimensional attributes of feature entities and value attributes of dimensional constraint entities. In many CAD systems real numerical parameters are uniformly treated as dimensions, and displayed to the designer as such.

ISO 10303-108 differentiates between independent and dependent parameters. The distinction arises in the use of the Part 108 entities **free_form_assignment** and **free_form_relation**, where independent parameters occur as reference elements and dependent parameters as constrained elements.

Column 5 distinguishes between cases where an implicit dimension is fully captured by a pure procedural representation and those where it is not. If all parameters can be captured implicitly by the use of an ISO 10303-42 [19] or --111 entity, data can be exchanged at Level 1, as defined earlier. If not, it will be necessary to use Level 2 or 3.

Table 2. Classification of "general" parameters of commercial CAD systems

Table 2-1: CAD system implicit parameters

Case 0	1	2	3	4	5		F	C	P
Case 1	Numeric	Bound	CAD system implicit dimension	CAD system implicit parameter	Free	Covered by Procedure	O	X	X
Case 2						Incomplete data	Δ	O	X
Case 3					Dependent	Covered by Procedure	O	X	O
Case 4						Incomplete data	Δ	O	O
Case 5					Independent	Covered by Procedure	O	X	O
Case 6						Incomplete data	Δ	O	O
Case 7			CAD system explicit dimension		Free		Δ	O	X
Case 8					Dependent		Δ	O	X
Case 9					Independent		Δ	O	X

Table 2-2: CAD system explicit parameters

Case 10	Numeric	Bound	CAD system explicit dimension	CAD system explicit parameter	Free		Δ	O	O
Case 11					Dependent		Δ	O	O
Case 12					Independent		Δ	O	O
Case 13		Unbound	N/A		Free		Δ	X	O
Case 14					Dependent		Δ	X	O
Case 15					Independent		Δ	X	O

Table 2-3: Redundant parameters

Case 16	Numeric	Redundant	Display	Dependent			X	X	X
Case 17			Fixed N/A				X	X	X

Table 2-4: Non-numeric parameters

Case 18	Non-Numeric			Covered by Procedure	O	X	X
Case 19				Incomplete data	Δ	O	X

In Table 2, the columns labeled F, C, P are concerned with the existence of feature, constraint and parameter entities in an ISO 10303 exchange file. If the entity need not be transmitted in the exchange file an "X" entry occurs in the relevant column. If the entity is obligatory for transmitting the parameter and its semantics then the entry is "O". The feature entities considered are those from ISO 10303-42 and -111. The dimension entities are those from ISO 10303-108 that have names ending in **_with_dimension**. The parameter entity is the **variational_parameter** entity in ISO 10303-108 and its instantiable subtypes.

In Case 1, all variables occur as attributes of feature creation operations defined in an instance of **procedural_solid_representation_sequence**, and are therefore obligatory. Case 2 covers situations where some variables (for example, positioning dimensions, if these are defined separately from the actual feature creation operation) are specified explicitly. In such a case the relevant feature entity is present in the exchange file, so that 'X' appears in column P, but 'Δ' also appears in Column F to indicate that additional information is needed.

Use of the **variational_parameter** entity from ISO 10303-108 is necessary for cases 3 – 6 in Table 2-1 and all cases in Table 2-2. In cases 3 – 6 it is needed to represent the variables in the equation. In Cases 2, 4, 6, 7 – 9 and 10 – 12 an ISO 10303-108 dimensional constraint should be used unless the dimension is implicit, having been created by a creation operation, when this is not necessary.

The 'redundant' cases 16 and 17 in Table 2 are not considered further, because they are concerned with dimensional information provided in the sending system purely for annotation and display purposes. Such information is irrelevant in the reconstruction of a model in the receiving system. If necessary, that system can derive dimensions as appropriate from the transferred model and reconstruct any desired annotation in its own native manner.

5.3 Constraint Interoperability

Commercial CAD systems appear to represent most sketch constraints explicitly, and these can be transferred using the explicit constraint capabilities of ISO 10303-108. As already mentioned, implicit constraints arise from the constructional operations defined in ISO 10303-42, -111 and -112. They are discussed further below. Analogous construction operations in different CAD system give rise to different results for constrained configurations in 3D; for example, in some cases implicitly created constraints are recorded explicitly in the model file, and in others they are not. Some systems store user-selected 3D reference elements for sketch constraints in 3D form; others project these reference elements onto the sketch plane if they are curves or intersect them with it if they are surfaces, and only store representations of the resulting 2D geometry.

An *implicit* or *procedural constraint* is a constraint that results automatically from the operation of a constructional procedure used in creating a model [6]. For example, a procedure 'create tangent line' may be used in a 2D procedural model. Its input is a curve (assumed to exist before the procedure is used) and a point. The output is a line through the point and tangent to the curve. In this case there is no explicit imposition of the tangency constraint by the user, and the constraint is not explicitly represented in the evaluated representation of the sketch as shown on the screen, although the *effect* of the constraint is evident in the screen display. The term *implicit dimension* has been used in a similar manner to denote a dimension that has not been explicitly created by the designer [29].

Table 3 below gives a classification, from the translator developer's point of view, of *directed* constraints, in which certain model elements (*constrained elements*) are constrained with respect to one or more *reference elements*. Column 2 specifies the context in which the constraint was created, and Column 3 specifies whether it is explicit or implicit. Column 4 specifies whether the reference elements are internal to the sketch, or what kind of data structure they belong to if they lie outside the sketch. The work reported here, which has been solely concerned with the exchange of part models, has dealt with constraints belonging to Cases 1 – 4 and Case 7 of the table. Cases 5 and 6 typically arise in the context of assembly models, and are outside the scope of the present work.

Table 3. Classification of directed constraints from the implementation point of view

Case	Where created	Type	Reference geometric elements
1	In the sketch context		Internal to the sketch
2			External B-rep elements
3		Explicit	Elements of another sketch
4			Datum elements outside the sketch
5		Implicit	Not considered in this work
6	Outside the sketch context	Explicit	Not considered in this work
7		Implicit	Situation-dependent

Dimensional and logical constraints comprise three main information elements: an identifier (ID), semantics, and target geometry. Any of these elements may give rise to constraint interoperability problems, as discussed below. In the ID case, for example, problems may arise because a constraint involving elements of a feature may have an ID that relates only to that particular feature rather than the overall model.

5.3.1 Constraint identifiers

Conceptually, explicit dimensions are either size dimensions or location dimensions. A size dimension is intrinsic to the geometry of a particular element in a sketch or feature; in some cases it may be specified with respect to an auxiliary geometric element such as a centerline. A location dimension is used in 2D to determine the relative location of a sketch element with respect to other elements, and in 3D to locate a feature with respect to a higher-level feature or a datum. Parts may also be positioned in assemblies using 3D location dimensions, but that application is outside the scope of the present paper. Inter-feature relationships in a CAD model may be very complex if long chains of locational dimensions occur.

Problems will inevitably arise if inter-feature constraints are not explicitly specified. As mentioned earlier, the automatic identification of implicit constraints is possible in principle, but dangerous in practice. The number of pairs of elements that have to be checked for possible constraint relationships will be very large for a complex CAD model, and the possibility of spurious detection of constraints arising from chance coincidences of position or orientation of model elements will be very high [26].

In the receiving system, the relation between a constraint and its owning feature must be determined through the transmitted ISO 10303 relations between the constraint and the geometric elements it involves. Post-processing requires the choice of the most appropriate mapping class for each feature concerned; this is determined by the granularity of the feature definition in the receiving system as compared with that of the ISO 10303-108 definition occurring in the exchange file, including all applicable dimensions and constraints.

In commercial CAD systems explicit constraints are associated with specific sketches or features, and unique identifiers are often allocated to them in the sketch or feature context. However, ISO 10303 defines no such association, and allocates unique identifiers in the exchange file at the part (or assembly) level. From the information in an ISO 10303 exchange file the feature or sketch owning the constraint must be identified as the one whose geometric elements are referenced by that constraint. Then the constraint set for a feature or sketch can be compiled by identifying all constraints referencing geometric elements associated with the construct of interest.

A sketch-based feature in ISO 1030-111 requires the underlying sketch to be provided as an instance of **face_surface.** Extrusion operations in CAD systems are mainly based on the use of sketches, but such systems create no constructs that map exactly to the sketch representations defined in Clause 7 of ISO 10303-108 [6], which are specified in a manner dictated by a requirement for upwards compatibility with other (earlier) ISO 10303 resources. The use of **face_surface** rules out the possibility that the sketch boundary is not closed, a case which requires specialized interpretation when used with an extrusion operation. Ideally, all constraints need to be correctly assigned to their owning features to ensure successful procedural transmission. If the reference geometry of a constraint is of Type 2 or Type 4 in Table 3 above, not associated with a specific sketch or feature, then it is necessary to scan all the geometry in the exchange file to find a match.

5.3.2 Semantic mapping of constraints

Semantics must be dealt with on a case-by-case basis. For example, a **vertical** direction constraint in one system may correspond to several different constraint possibilities both in another CAD system and in the ISO 10303 exchange file, as shown in Table 4 below. Translator writers need to consider multiple possibilities for semantic mappings, not only between the sending system and the exchange file, but also between the exchange file and the receiving system. It is important to capture and transfer the maximal amount of information to allow for diverse representations of that information following the transfer.

Table 4 shows some possibilities for constraining a line to be vertical in a sketch. In the sending system, the 'same coordinate' constraint requires the x coordinates of the two ends of a line segment to be equal. A second alternative is the use of a 'vertical' constraint, and a third requires the line to be perpendicular to another line which is horizontal. ISO 10303-108 does not provide a 'vertical' constraint; it would be normal to create a 2D vector or direction (0, 1) in the exchange file and require the line to be parallel to that. Alternatively, a 'perpendicular' constraint could be used as in the sending system, the reference element now being a vector or direction (1, 0). The effect of the 'same coordinate' constraint is also available in ISO 10303-108. In the transfer illustrated by the table, the particular receiving system concerned will in all three cases reconstruct the constraint as 'vertical.'

Table 4. Example of semantic differences between constraints

Sending	Neutral [Part 108]	Receiving
same_coordinate	several solutions available (e.g., **equal_parameter_constraint**)	vertical
vertical parallel	(to something else that is vertical in the sketch)	vertical
perpendicular (to something that is horizontal in the sketch)	perpendicular (to something that is horizontal in the sketch)	vertical

5.3.3 Constrained and reference elements

Constraints may be applied between the geometric elements of a sketch, and also between sketch elements and other geometric elements external to the sketch context. This last capability is useful, for example, in packaging applications where it is necessary to fit the parameterized shape of some component into an enclosure defined by fixed external geometry [24]. Some CAD systems allow constraints to be applied between geometric elements belonging to different sketches, but others do not.

In exceptional cases, constraints may be applied between sketch elements and other elements that do not exist explicitly in the model, and this makes pure procedural parametric data exchange more complex. For example, some CAD systems allow the imposition of constraints with respect to 2D geometry defined implicitly by projection of some 3D element onto a sketch plane. ISO 10303-108 provides representations for several types of implicitly defined curves for use as reference elements in sketch constraints in these situations.

5.3.4 Mathematical equation interoperability

The terminology used for algebraically defined constraints differs between CAD systems, but the principles are the same. The most important aspect of the transfer of expressions or equations is the correct mapping of the dimensional or other parameters involved. The identifiers of these parameters can be identified in the sending system by parsing the equation or expression, which is normally represented there as a character string. For reasons of upwards compatibility such constructs are represented in an ISO 10303 exchange file in terms of individual operator and operand entities, but it is easy to map between the two types of representation.

5.4 Geometric interoperability

5.4.1 User-selected elements

An important problem arising in the exchange of procedural or construction history models is that of identifying, in the exchange file, geometric model elements that were selected in the sending system by a screen pick by the system user. A related difficulty, arising in the context of model editing within a single CAD system, is known as the *persistent naming problem* [30]. The problem proves to be less acute for data exchange, because the intention is to regenerate an exactly similar model in the receiving system rather than a modification of the model. ISO 10303-55 provides a mechanism for the identification of selected elements that relies on the transmission of one or more explicit elements in traditional ISO 10303 mode [9, 23].

5.4.2 The geometric accuracy problem

In a parametric model there are many possibilities for inconsistency arising from geometric accuracy problems. Some of these are concerned with the values used to define the geometric elements of the model, but others relate to design intent information. For example, it is possible that dimensional values relating feature elements are inconsistent with the actual geometrical definitions of those elements, or that geometric constraints such as parallelism or tangency are not exactly satisfied by the geometry as defined in the model. It is usual to judge that a particular configuration is consistently defined if any measured inconsistency is less than the value of some geometric tolerance. However, different CAD systems use different values for their internal geometric tolerances, and some define a wider range of different tolerance types (on distances, angles, etc.) than others. The effects of geometric inaccuracies can propagate and increase in magnitude as modeling proceeds, particularly when inaccurately computed geometry conflicts with specified topology. In the transfer of boundary representation solids, topological information is usually regarded as having precedence over geometry. In a similar manner, constraint information, when present, usually takes precedence over representations of individual geometric elements.

The work reported in the current paper does not address the geometric accuracy problem in any general sense, but concentrates on its effects in the procedural model as defined in the sending system. In their work on the identification and correction of errors in the exchange of CAD shape models Hong Gu et al. [11] found that structural errors and accuracy errors have a smaller effect when procedural model exchange is used than they do in the exchange of explicit B-rep models.

A procedural model to be transmitted contains no explicit Class 1 geometry. That class of geometry exists only in the redundant associated B-rep model. In CAD systems, the other three classes of geometric elements defined earlier may be regarded, for translation purposes, as excluding all purely topological elements. Such elements may sometimes be created in those classes, but generally without sufficient information to allow a full ISO 10303 description to be generated in the exchange file. Class 2 and Class 4 geometric elements provide supporting information for constructional procedures but are not involved in topological relationships, and Class 3 elements occur in sketches that do not contain topology. Thus (if we exclude the dual transmission of the secondary B-rep model), all geometry exchanged in a procedural parametric data exchange using the hypothetical ISO 10303 Application Protocol mentioned earlier consists of sketch elements, selected elements, and auxiliary supporting or constructional elements.

In the case of Class 3 sketch geometry, a constraint may assert that one end-point of a given line coincides with one end-point of a given arc. In the model as actually transferred, the geometry may not satisfy the specified constraint because of numerical errors resulting from geometric computations. The presence of the constraint in the transferred model will alert the receiving system to the fact that the two elements should meet as specified. In principle, the constraint has precedence over the geometric information. However, ISO 10303-108 does not specify behavior of the receiving system. Whether or not it rectifies the situation to restore consistency, and if so, how it performs the rectification, is a matter for that system. If rectification occurs, it may give rise to minor inconsistencies between the explicit models as transmitted from the sending system and as reconstructed in the receiving system.

Experience suggests the following set of guidelines for avoiding or minimizing geometric accuracy problems.

1. Features or logical constraints should be used, wherever possible, to avoid the use of numerical values or dimensions. This gives the maximal capture of design intent and reduces possibility of geometric accuracy problems.
2. The optimal setting of session parameters should be used in creating a model that is to be exchanged with another system. Most systems provide many such parameters. It will be necessary to define user guidelines for each type of CAD system, recommending the most appropriate settings for the data exchange of procedural models. The choices available to the user usually include the following relevant settings:
   ○ *the use of a grid in sketching* – this allows only the choice of a discrete set of points and angular orientations for sketch elements;
   ○ *the use of shaded model renderings* – this may not allow the screen selection of hidden entities in the model;
   ○ *the use of automatically generated constraints*, which may be accepted by the user and stored as part of the model data.
3. In the case of a non-closed sketch used to define a 'cut' feature (Boolean subtraction), extensions should be provided at the end-points of the sketch cross-section to avoid problems in computing the sketch intersection with the part boundary.
4. The constructional strategy used should be carefully considered. In particular, the number of datums and user-selected reference elements should be kept to a minimum, consistent with any desired parent-child relationships between features. These relationships constitute an important part of design intent for the part model, and affect its behavior under modification. However, the handling of datums and selected elements is

one of the more difficult and computationally intensive aspects of CAD data exchange. Any admissible simplification in this respect will lead to simpler and more accurate translation.

5.4.3 Preservation of selected geometry

As mentioned above, an explicit geometric constraint has three parts: (1) an identifier (ID), (2) a specification or descriptive semantics (which in dimensional cases will involve a parameter value), and (3) details of the constrained geometry. Some CAD systems only allow binary constraints, in which the number of geometric elements involved is limited to two. In this case if designer selects $N > 2$ geometric elements then $N - 1$ binary constraints are created. The elements involved in a geometric constraint are either *reference elements* or *constrained elements*. A reference element is a model element to which constrained elements are related by a directed constraint, and a constrained element is one that is controlled by the constraint if the model is edited following a transfer into another system. A constraint with one or more reference elements is said to be a *directed constraint*. In contrast, an *undirected constraint* has no reference elements and requires the constrained condition to hold amongst all pairs of members of a set of constrained elements [6].

A CAD system API, when queried for the geometric elements involved in a constraint, may return either the system names of those elements or direct pointers to the elements themselves.

For sketch constraints, explicit information concerning the geometric elements involved is generally available via the API of the CAD system. For non-sketch constraints, different systems represent the relevant information in different ways. In the case of an implicit constraint outside the sketch context, the nature of the constraint may be inferred from the definition of the feature concerned. Although some CAD systems do not allow the definition of 3D constraints within a part model, the effect may be achieved indirectly, for example, by the creation of a datum element based on an element of one feature that is used in definition of a second feature. This implies a 3D relationship between the two features concerned, but it is not represented explicitly as a constraint in the CAD system. In an ISO 10303 exchange file, however, the possibility exists for expressing this relationship by an equivalent explicit constraint.

Table 5. Element types for the primary geometric constraint entities defined in ISO 10303-108
(Abbreviations: agce = **axial_geometry_constraint_element**;
csce = **curve_or_surface_constraint_element**;
gce = **geometric_constraint_element**; gri = **geometric_representation_item**;
lgce = **linear_geometry_constraint_element**;
pcsce = **point_curve_or_surface_constraint_element**;
rge = **radial_geometry_constraint_element**)

TYPE of Constraint Entity Constrained		Reference
fixed_element_geometric_constraint	SET[1:?] OF gce	—
parallel_geometric_constraint	SET[1:?] OF lgce	SET[0:1] OF lgce
point_distance_geometric_constraint	SET[1:?] OF **point**	SET[0:4] OF pcsce

skew_line_distance_geometric_constraint	SET[1:2] OF line	SET[0:1] OF line
curve_distance_geometric_constraint SET[1:2]	of **curve** SET[0:4]	OF pcsce
surface_distance_geometric_constraint SET[1:?]	OF **surface** SET[0:4]	OF pcsce
radius_geometric_constraint	SET[1:?] OF rgce	—
curvelengthgeometricconstraint	SET[1:?] OF boundedcurve	—
parallel_offset_geometric_constraint SET[1:?]	OF csce	SET[0:1] OF csce
angle_geometric_constraint SET[1:?] OF	lgce	SET[0:1] OF lgce
perpendicular_geometric_constraint	SET[1:?] OF lgce	SET[0:2] OF lgce
incidence_geometric_constraint	SET[1:?] OF gce	SET[0:?] OF gce
coaxial_geometric_constraint SET[1:?] OF	agce	SET[0:1] OF agce
tangent_geometric_constraint	SET[1:?] OF csce	SET[0:?] OF csce
symmetry_geometric_constraint SET[2:2]	OF gri	—

Some other considerations regarding the geometry of constraint elements are briefly discussed below:

○ *Geometry in the neutral file* : ISO 10303-108 requires constraints to reference the underlying geometry of constrained topological elements (points, curves, surfaces — see Table 5). In some cases it is necessary to refer to the defining elements of geometrical entities rather than the entities themselves. For example, if it is desired to constrain a cylindrical surface to be perpendicular to a plane it is necessary to formulate the constraint in terms of the axial direction of the cylinder rather than the actual cylindrical surface. This approach allows the total number of constraint types to be reduced because specialized constraint types do not have to be defined for each specific type of geometrical entity. On the other hand, the referencing of defining elements of constrained curves and surfaces rather than the curves and surfaces themselves creates more difficulties in the implementation of translators because the references to constrained elements are indirect [18]. An example is the ISO 10303-108 requirement to reference the underlying circle when representing a constraint on an arc lying on that circle.

○ *Indeterminate geometric extent:* This problem often occurs when a datum element is output from the sending system to a STEP file. Datum elements are usually defined by the CAD system with default dimensions, though in some cases no dimension is specified. For example, a datum plane may be displayed by a CAD system with default dimensions of 100 × 100 units, and it may be represented internally with that precise size and the topology of a face, or as an unbounded plane that is displayed as finite for easier understanding by the designer. In either case the program that writes the exchange file should create appropriate geometry to enable the exchange file reader to reconstruct the relationship involving the datum correctly from the point of view of the receiving system. Initial experience suggests that the most appropriate type of geometry to transfer for a datum is the most general – for example, unbounded lines, planes, etc. rather than bounded ones.

○ *Compatible geometry in the CAD system:* It is possible for an entity that is not itself a sketch segment to possess a system ID in the context of the sketch. For example, if a circular arc is defined as a visible sketch element, the underlying circle definition may be stored as an invisible element. It is then possible to apply a radial dimension constraint to the circle, which will apply indirectly to the arc. Another example is shown in Fig. 5. Here the sketch mode of the CAD system only supports 2D elements in the sketch plane, which is the plane containing the edges E1 and E2. If the user positions the center of the circle used to define the protrusion feature with respect to face F1, the system will instead use the edge E1 as the reference element because it lies in the sketch plane while F1 is a 3D element that does not.

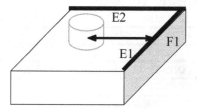

Fig. 5 Example of compatible geometry as constraint target

○ *Indirect selection of geometry in the neutral file:*   In this case, a higher-level model element is selected indirectly in terms of one or more lower-level entities that are used to define it. Examples are the selection of two of its edges to distinguish a selected face, or the selection of a feature face as representative of an entire feature to be modified. Such indirect selections may be represented in an ISO 10303 exchange file using the entity **indirectly_selected_elements** defined in ISO 10303-55.

○ *Use of a point to represent a selected element:*   This technique refers to a selected geometric element in terms of a characteristic point that is not part of the defining data. For example, a selected edge may be referenced via its mid-point, which is likely to identify it uniquely in the model. Mun used this method for identifying selected elements in the exchange file in an early stage of his translator implementation [21]. However, it was found that identification of the desired geometric element and its ID from the full list of geometric elements in the model file was very computationally intensive. Although easy to implement, the method is also very susceptible to geometric accuracy problems.

○ *Change of reference:* In a sketch, even if the user references a plane as the reference element for a constraint, a CAD system will usually represent the constraint in terms of a compatible reference line.

○ *Choice of lines or planes as reference elements:*   For non-sketch constraints, linear edges of the model are often used as reference elements for positioning and orienting features, rather than planes. Whether or not this is appropriate depends upon the semantics of the constraint, but in cases where no ambiguity arises, it is generally acceptable.

○ *Dimensionality of constraint elements:* ISO 10303 does not allow mixed dimensionality in any of its representations. Thus in a 3D model, a line used as a datum must have dimensionality 3, i.e. it must exist in the 3D space of the model rather than the 2D space of a sketch.

○ *User selected elements in an exchange file:*   Any element(s) selected by the user from the screen is marked in an exchange file by an instance of the ISO 10303-55 entity **user_selected_elements**. Such elements will often not belong to the final B-rep, having been modified or deleted by subsequent operations.

○ *Representation of datums in an exchange file:*   Datums will often be recorded in a procedural model as explicit points, lines or planes that provide supporting information for a constructional operation occurring in a **procedural_solid_representation_-sequence**. If a datum is not part of the model geometry but is used as the reference element in a constraint used to position or orient a feature then the Part 108 entity **auxiliary_geometric_representation_item** is available for its representation.

Suggested guidelines for the preservation of selected geometry are as follows:

1. In pre-processing, before creating geometry for a constraint in the exchange file, a check should be made to determine whether a geometric element that can be used for the intended purpose has already been written into the file.
2. In post-processing, duplication of elements used in constraints should be avoided; if a suitable element already exists, it should be used.
3. In the pure procedural approach to sketch representation (i.e., where a sketch is not transmitted explicitly in the exchange file), it is best to create all the geometric elements of a sketch first and then to define constraints between them, rather than alternating between element creation and constraint definition. This is because the sketch elements adjust themselves each time a new constraint is added. Hence the selection of an element part through the alternating type of approach makes it more difficult to identify the selected element once the sketch is complete. The element concerned may have possibly been modified several times since its initial selection, as a result of further constraint definitions.

An example of the application of Guideline 2 above occurs when the centerline of an axisymmetric feature is used as the reference for a linear dimension, and the center-line was automatically created with the feature. No copy of that center-line should be created for dimensioning purposes; the original should be used. In ISO 10303-42 the center-line of a feature generated by revolving a sketch is defined as an instance of **axis1_placement_2d**. This requires two elements of support geometry, of types **point** and **direction**. Often, a constraint between two such center-lines may be formulated in more than one way in the exchange file, in terms of a relation between the two defining points, or the two defining directions, or between two instances of line that can be constructed using the defining data of the two instances of **axis1_placement_2d**. The choice will depend on the CAD system generating the initial information, and it should be made in such a way that information transfer is maximized. In general, constraints formulated between elements of supporting geometry are harder to implement and interpret, while constraints between redundant constructed geometric elements result in verbose files and possible geometric inconsistency.

6. IMPLEMENTATION AND CASE STUDIES

6.1 Translator implementation

Table 6 below shows the notation used in the following discussion.

Table 6. Notation for description of implementation

Symbol	Meaning
F_i	i th Feature
P	Parameter (explicit)
D	Dimension
C	Constraint
H	History of construction

G_i	Geometry and Topology
B_i	B-rep after addition of i th feature
X	Explicit element
M	Model
R	Relation
A	Attribute array (includes implicit parameters)

Where feature-based design has been used to create the part model, its procedural representation is essentially a list of features. In what follows we will use M to denote a model, and F a feature. The suffix $_s$ distinguishes elements of information in the sending system, while suffix $_e$ denotes elements as exported to the exchange file. The symbol Y in Equation 1-1 denotes a generalized Boolean union, the result of a succession of I feature creation operations, each performed on the pre-existing version of the part model. Most other information elements in the model (dimensions, constraints, etc.) may be considered to be integral to feature definitions. There are four exceptions in a model of a single part: (1) relations between two features, (2) relations between two elements belonging to different features, (3) relations defined in a design family table, and (4) information about session parameters used during the modeling process. None of these are defined at the feature level. The last type of information is only relevant for model exchange insofar as it may affect the accuracy or completeness of the transmitted model data (see Section 4.4.1 above). If we take 'relation' to indicate either an equation defined in the CAD model itself or a relation specified in a design family table, then we can express the model file in the sending system as a feature list plus a relation set:

$$M_S(F_S, R_S) = F_S + R_S = \bigcup_{i=1}^{I} F_{S_i} + \sum_{q=1}^{Q} R_{S_q} \quad (1\text{-}1)$$

where

$$F_{S_i} = F_{S_i}(A_i, G_{S_i}, H_{S_i}, D_{S_i}, C_{S_i}) \quad (1\text{-}2, 1\text{-}3)$$
$$R_{S_q} = R_{S_q}(A_q)$$

The feature pointer gives access to the defining geometry (G), history (H), dimensions (D), constraints (C) and related attributes (A) of each feature. From the relation pointer we can get the related attributes (A_q), mainly in the form of strings representing equations. Such strings need to be parsed for identification of the dimensional or other parameters they contain. Some examples of system-specific equation strings are "P8 = D19*D19 + 4*D19 – 5" (Pro/Engineer®) and "D1@Sketch4" = "D2@Sketch4" *"D2@Sketch4" + 4*"D2@Sketch4" – 5 (Solidworks®).

Each operation sequence is expressed in the ISO 10303 exchange file as an instance of the ISO 10303-55 entity **procedural_solid_representation_sequence**. One or more instances of this entity can participate in an instance of the ISO 10303-55 entity **procedural_shape_representation**, which may represent an entire part history, and may be expressed as follows:

$$M_E(F_E, R_E) = F_E + D_E + R_E = \bigcup_{i=1}^{I} F_{Ei} + \sum_{j=1}^{J} D_{Ej} + \sum_{q=1}^{Q} R_{Eq}$$

$$F_{Ei} = F_{Ei}(A_i, G_{Ei}, H_{Ei}, C_{Ei})$$

$$D_{Ej} = D_{Ej}(A_j, F_{Ej}, X_{Ej})$$

$$R_{Eq} = R_{Eq}(A_q, D_{Eq}, P_{Eq})$$

$$(2\text{-}1 - 2\text{-}4)$$

There are some general technical requirements for implementations. Uniform temporary data structures are necessary for lists of objects of various types. For example, a geometric constraint may have reference geometry of type line, arc, datum axis or datum plane, etc., so that it is convenient and efficient to implement a single data structure that can accommodate all the relevant types. This should take into account ISO 10303 supertype/subtype relationships for such elements. The programs that write and read the exchange file then have access to all salient model elements by using pointers for traversing the list of features in the model, and the lists of dimensions, constraints and algebraic relations at the individual feature level. During translation three data structures are open simultaneously: those of the CAD system, the program writing or reading the exchange file, and the neutral file. This is necessary, for example, to establish correspondences between the different identifiers used in the sending system and in the ISO 10303 exchange file for the elements involved in a constraint. Geometric elements should be translated before constraints, because they may be referenced multiple times by dimensional or other constraints, especially in the sketch context.

For some CAD systems, the use of Eqs. 2, based on the exchange file structure, may lead to a simpler translator implementation than Eqs. 1, based on the native model structure. Eqs. 2 require the generation of a redundant dimension data structure for convenience in retrieving dimensions, which is beneficial if that proves to be a frequent requirement. The problem here is related to the feature granularity issue. If there are dimensions associated with a feature in the sending system that are not implicitly accounted for in the ISO 10303-111 representation of that feature (i.e., that representation has smaller granularity), then those additional dimensions must be written into the exchange file as instances of explicit ISO 10303-108 dimensional entities. This involves a search of the model to identify the particular geometric elements related by each explicit dimension. These occur as attributes of dimensional constraint instances, and it is these attributes that must be searched. In the sending system, dimensions and other parameters, together with any equations that relate them, are often scattered between individual owning feature representations rather than held centrally for the model as a whole. Thus the search process is greatly simplified by the generation of a temporary array of dimensions for the model as a whole, providing capabilities for indexing dimensionally constrained geometric elements to individual features.

Eq. (2-1) represents the normalized data structure in the sending system. From Eq. 2-4 it can be seen that R_E is a function of the dimensions and possibly other non-dimensional parameters. That implies that even though the translation of a feature may be complete, the dimension and parameter data are still in use, and therefore information needs to be processed in the order implied by Equation 2-1.

Equation (1-2) for the native model in the sending system corresponds to Eqs. (2-2) and (2-3) for the exchange file. In the sending system the generation of constraint arrays for each feature is not appropriate, because constraints may be used outside the feature context. However, dimensions and parameters may be related by equations. Unless the corresponding arrays for these entities exist, it may be necessary to scan every feature in the model to find a single dimension, which is very time-consuming.

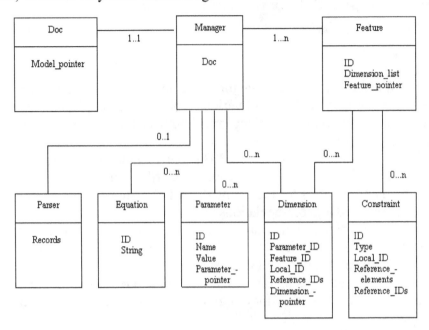

Fig. 6. Class diagram for translator implementation

For two-way exchange between two CAD systems four translators are needed: programs for reading and writing the exchange file for both systems. The processors developed are based on the classes shown Fig. 6. The " **Doc**" class is an encapsulation of the "model pointer" of the CAD file, which provides access to all the other classes. The role of the " **Manager**" class is to manage access to lower-level data structures such as feature lists, equation sets, dimension and constraint sets and parameter sets. The class " **Parser**" is concerned with STEP file parsing. The module concerned was developed *ab initio* for the work described in this paper, but a commercial parsing library could alternatively be used. The class structure shown captures the basic structure of a typical CAD system API, and so it can be used for the development of processors for other CAD systems. It could be further developed into a standardized high level API for developing ISO 10303 translators.

6.2 Case Studies

ISO 10303-108 contains eight clauses, of which the first three contain preliminary information and the last five the main content. The following examples illustrate the usage of clauses 4 through 8 of this new part of STEP. The test parts used were all taken from Pro/Engineer ® tutorial material and related sources. All the transferred models were found to exhibit satisfactory variation under editing in the receiving system.

Before presenting the case studies it is necessary to explain the structure of the ISO 10303 exchange file as defined in ISO 10303-21 ('Clear text encoding of the exchange structure'). A STEP Application Protocol, relating to a specific product type and product life-cycle stage, defines the entity types that occur in an exchange. Each defined entity is characterized by a set of attributes, which may have values of various types. The exchange file consists primarily of a set of instances of the defined entity types, each instance having a unique identifier in the file which has the form of a integer number preceded by a hash character '#'. Each instance is specified by the name of the entity type concerned (in upper case) followed, in parentheses, by the list of values of the attributes for the particular instance concerned. If these attributes have 'simple' types (real, integer, Boolean or character string, for example) they are given explicitly. However, some attributes may have values defined by other instances in the file, and in that case they are specified in terms of the relevant instance identifier. For example, an unbounded line is defined in terms of a point and a direction. A line instance in the file will therefore contain references to an instance of a point and an instance of a direction. It is hoped that this explanation will make the following examples reasonably self-explanatory. Many details have been omitted, and ISO 10303-21 should be referred to for further information. Although ASCII file exchange is used for illustrative purposes in the case studies, it should be noted that ISO 10303 provides several other methods for the exchange and sharing of product information.

Case study 1: A sketch with explicit geometric constraints and dimensions, illustrating the capabilities of clauses 7 and 8 of ISO 10303-108:

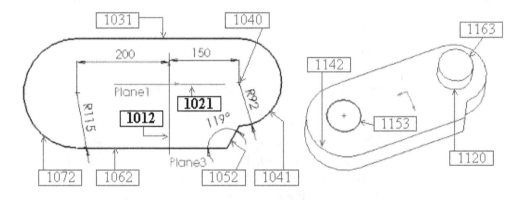

Fig. 7. 2D sketch and a solid derived from it

The base shape of the model is a linear extrusion of a sketch that was initially created on a datum plane. Two features are defined upon the base shape, a circular protrusion and a circular depression, both having the same radius. In the originating system (Pro/Engineer®), the constraints defined are 5 point coincidences, 3 tangencies, 2 horizontal direction constraints and 5 dimensions. Additionally, there is one 'same (x) coordinate' constraint between the center point of the arc R92 and the lower end point of that arc.

Table 7 shows a fragment of the ISO 10303 exchange file for the object shown in Fig. 7. Not all the instances referred to below are shown in the table. The ones missing from the table are shown in Fig. 7. The five incidence constraints are imposed on endpoints of successive curve segments making up the initial sketch, to ensure that it defines a continuous closed boundary. The three tangent constraints ensure smooth junctions between line segments and arcs in the sketch. ISO 10303-108 does not define the 'horizontal' constraint available in the CAD system, and the effect is achieved here by constraining the two long line segments to be parallel to #1021, a line instance (shown in Fig. 7 but not in Table 7) that has the required direction, using **parallel_geometric_constraint**. Section 3-3 of Table 7 contains the dimensional

43

constraints for the arc radii and the angle specified in the sketch. Section 3-4 contains the dimensional constraint specifying the distance from the center point #1071 of the arc #1072 to the datum plane 3.

Table 7. Fragment of ISO 10303-21 exchange file for constraints in the sketch shown in Fig. 7

3-1	#1081= TANGENT_GEOMETRIC_CONSTRAINT ('',(#1031,#1041),( )); #1082= TANGENT_GEOMETRIC_CONSTRAINT ('',(#1031,#1072), ( )); #1083= TANGENT_GEOMETRIC_CONSTRAINT ('',(#1062,#1072), ( ));
3-2	#1084= PARALLEL_GEOMETRIC_CONSTRAINT ('',(#1031),(#1021)); #1085= PARALLEL_GEOMETRIC_CONSTRAINT ('', (#1062),(#1021));
3-3	#1088= RGC_WITH_DIMENSION ('',(#1041), 92.0); #1089=AGC_WITH_DIMENSION('', (#1052, #1062), 119); #1090= RGC_WITH_DIMENSION ('',(#1072), 115.0);
3-4	#1092= PDGC_WITH_DIMENSION('', (#1071), (#1012),200.0);
3-5	#1091= PDGC_WITH_DIMENSION('', (#1040, #1037), (#1012),150.0);
3-6	#1125=RGC_WITH_DIMENSION ('',(#1120), 50.0);
3-7	#1167=COAXIAL_GEOMETRIC_CONSTRAINT('', (#1142),(#1153)); #1168=RADIUS_GEOMETRIC_CONSTRAINT ('', (#1163,#1153),());

In all the above cases ISO 10303-108 provides constraints that are compatible with the constraints in the model in the originating system. However, section 3-5 of Table 7 shows an example of an aggregation mapping, necessary because of differences in granularity. An instance of the constraint **pdgc_with_dimension** (point distance constraint with dimension) is shown, with reference element #1012, constrained elements #1037, #1040, and distance value 150. This constraint requires that the center and lower end-points of the arc are both distant 150 units from the vertical line #1012. This is compatible with, but not identical with, the intention in the originating system, which imposed a dimensional and a same-coordinate constraint. Thus, in this case two constraints in the sending system have been mapped to a single constraint in the ISO 10303 exchange file. An example of the reverse situation, where one constraint must be mapped onto more than one, occurs with the mid-point constraint commonly implemented in CAD systems but not provided in ISO 10303-108. Its effect may be achieved by using an instance of **incidence_geometric_constraint** to constrain three points to lie on a line, together with an instance of **point_distance_geometric_constraint** to constrain one of them to be equidistant from the other two [6].

In Section 3-6 of Table 7, instance #1125 represents an explicit radial dimension for the profile #1120 of the circular protrusion. Similarly, in Section 3-7, #1168 is the radial dimension of the profile #1153 of the cylindrical hole feature, which is coaxial with the cylindrical end of the outer profile. In both cases the coaxiality constraint may use as its reference element, equivalently, either a selected element (Class 2 geometry), a sketch segment (Class 3) or an auxiliary element (Class 4). Regarding constraint instance #1167, the Pro/Engineer® API function for the coaxial constraint uses the underlying circle as the reference element rather than the profile arc #1142 shown in Fig. 7. Either is equally valid in principle, and this illustrates a case where different but compatible elements may be used. However, it

44

may be easier for the receiving system to determine the matching element in the model under reconstruction there if the full arc definition is referenced rather than its underlying geometry. If the program writing the exchange file writes the underlying circle into the file the receiving system can still probably identify the appropriate model element indirectly, though additional problems will arise if, for example, there are two or more arc segments in the model all lying on the same circle. This example shows the advantage of transmitting the maximum possible amount of information in the interests of resolving ambiguities in model reconstruction.

The constraint instance #1168 requires the radii of the circle instances #1153 and #1163 to be equal. Instance #1120 could have been selected rather than #1163, because the result is equivalent. From the STEP physical file we cannot differentiate whether #1120 is a segment of a positioned sketch or a feature edge, because STEP uses the same data structure for both, whereas in most CAD systems, features and sketches are represented and managed using different data structures, with and without topology, respectively.

Case study 2: Treatment of an implicit dimensional constraint outside the sketch context (Clause 7 of ISO 10303-108)

In the ISO 10303-21 file fragment in Table 8 below, the **axis1_placement** instance #1130 defines the axis of a feature of revolution. In the sending system, a dimension of 1750 units was imposed between the axis of the revolved feature and the axis of the first of the cylindrical holes in the pattern, the particular system concerned having created both axes implicitly (though other systems would require their explicit creation). ISO 10303-108 requires that this dimension is represented as a distance between parallel lines, and the **axis1_placement** instances provide the necessary points and directions for these lines to be constructed and written into the file as instances #2001, #2002 (not shown in the file fragment). These are constrained to be parallel and to have the required separation by the dimensional constraint instance #1134.

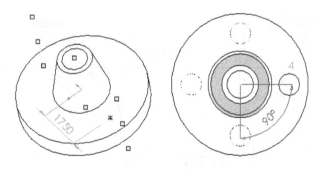

Fig. 8. Feature and pattern example

The three numerical values shown in Fig. 7 existed in a "dimension" data structure in the sending system. The two values shown in the second subfigure of Fig. 8 are not user-created dimensions; they were created automatically by a pattern creation operation that led to implicit definition of the hole circle radius and the angular spacing. However, in this case the sending system wrote the corresponding explicit dimensions into a dimensional data structure.

Case study 3: A pattern of features with parameterization and constraints (clause 4 of ISO 10303-108)

In this part, the diameter attribute of the circle of holes is important. It can be calculated as twice the radius dimension shown in the first subfigure of Fig. 8. The last section of Table 8 shows the ISO 10303 encoding of an explicit mathematical constraint ensuring this relationship, using a capability defined in clause 5 of ISO 10303-108. For historical reasons this requires mathematical expressions and relationships to be expressed in a parsed form in terms of individual operators and operands, rather than in a string form as in most scientific programming languages and CAD systems. The particular example shown concerns the association of two parameters, one with the radius of the bolt hole circle (an implicit dimension used in positioning the initial circle in the pattern) and the other with its diameter. The ISO 10303-108 entity **free_form_relation** is used to constrain the second to have twice the value of the first; the first attribute of instance #1187 in the file fragment specifies the set of constrained elements (the two parameters) and the last attribute specifies the required relationship between them. There are some complexities in the last section of the file fragment that are not explained here; details may be found in [24].

Table 8. Fragment of STEP file illustrating use of parameters and constraints outside the sketch context.

```
#1130=AXIS1_PLACEMENT('CENTER_LINE',#1131, #1132);
#1131=PLACEMENT('',#1133);
#1132=DIRECTION ('AXIS1', (0,-1,0));
#1133=CARTESIAN_POINT('',0,268.75,0);
```
```
#1134=PGC_WITH_DIMENSION('HOLE.64.PLACEMENT','',( #2001),( #2002), 1750);
```
```
#1135=AXIS_PLACEMENT_3D('AXIS_3D', #1136, #1137, #1138);
#1136=DIRECTION('HOLE.64(Z)',0, -1, 0);
#1137=DIRECTION('HOLE.64(X)',-1, 0, 0);
#1138=CARTESIAN_POINT('',175, 93.75, 2.29614e-015);
```
```
#1139=DESIGN_ROUND_HOLED_SOLID('HOLE.64', #1135, 37.5, 10);
```
```
#1144=AXIS2_PLACEMENT_3D('AXIS_3D', #1147, #1145, #1146);
#1145=DIRECTION('HOLE.64(Z)',0, -1, 0);
#1146=DIRECTION('HOLE.64(X)',0.545673, -0.837998, 7.15966e-018);
#1147=CARTESIAN_POINT('',0, 268.75, 0);
#1148=DESIGN_CIRCULAR_PATTERN_SOLID('PATTERN.64', #1139, #1144, 90, .FALSE., 4);
```
```
#1176=FINITE_REAL_INTERVAL(*, CLOSED, *, CLOSED);
#1177=BOUND_VARIATIONAL_PARAMETER('P1',#1176, *,'D 9', *);
#1178=FINITE_REAL_INTERVAL(*, CLOSED, *, CLOSED);
#1179=UNBOUND_VARIATIONAL_PARAMETER
('P2',#1178, *,'BOLT_CIRCLE_DIA', *);
#1180 = INSTANCE_ATTRIBUTE_REFERENCE
('EXPLICIT_GEOMETRIC_CONSTRAINT_SCHEMA.PGC_WITH_DIMENSION.DISTANCE_VALUE',
#1134);
#1181=PARAMETRIC_ENVIRONMENT( #1177, #1180);
```

```
#1182=REAL_LITERAL(1);
#1183=MULT_EXPRESSION(#1182, #1178);
#1184=REAL_LITERAL(2);
#1185=DIVIDE_EXPRESSION(#1183, #1184);
#1186=COMPARISON_EQUAL((#1177, #1185);
#1187=FREE_FORM_RELATION((#1177, #1179), () , #1186);
```

In general, the most important aspect of equation translation is the correct mapping of parameters. The system identifiers used for those parameters by the individual systems are irrelevant, because CAD systems use different conventions for assigning names. The parameters are therefore referred to only by 'neutral' instance numbers in the ISO 10303 exchange file, and appropriate new names will be assigned to them by the receiving system when they are regenerated there.

Relationships between dimensions or parameters are represented by CAD systems as specialized strings. The preprocessing phase involves parsing a string in the sending system to determine what parameters it contains and the forms of the relationships between them. Effectively, the exchange file will then contain a parsed version of the original string, which must be encoded in tree form in the exchange file and then reconstructed in the appropriate new string form in the receiving system.

It is desirable to deal with mathematical relations in the final stage of translation, because such constraints on parameters and dimensions are frequently not created until after the initial generation of feature geometry. The appropriate ordering is therefore geometry, followed by parameters/dimensions, and finally relations.

Case study 4: Verification that a parametric change in the received model generates another member of the same variational family (Clause 6 of ISO 10303-108)

Fig. 9 shows a master model (the model shown in Fig. 8) as transmitted between systems, and some members of the same part family generated in the receiving system by changing values of some of the ten independent parameters in the model. The model also contained some dependent parameters, which were correctly reevaluated in the receiving system according to transmitted constraint relationships. All the degrees of freedom in the model were tested, and no incorrect results were generated. This case study demonstrates the outstanding advantage of parametric data exchange — the ability to modify a model after transmission in accordance with the designer's original intentions.

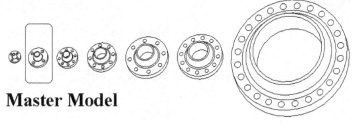

Master Model

Fig 9. Model used for Part Family case study

47

Some CAD systems create a table that displays all the independent parameters and specifies mathematical relations (including inequalities and conditional relationships) between parameters (see Table 9). Because of lack of functionality in the APIs of some CAD systems the transmission and regeneration of such tables is performed semi-automatically at the time of writing, some information being manually transferred from an intermediate spreadsheet application.

Table 9. Fragment of design family table for part family

	Axis-hole distance	Hole diameter	Blending radius	Number of bolt holes	6 more parameters...
N3	1.75	0.75	0.10625	4	...
N12	5.25	1.125	0.4375	12	...
....	..				

7. CONCLUSIONS

This paper presents foundations for the standardized exchange of parameterized shape construction history models between different CAD systems. The primary issues discussed are those concerned with classification, structuring and interoperability in the use of recent enhancements to ISO 10303, the STEP standard. Classification allows the choice of the most appropriate approach to the transfer of specific types of information, structuring helps to prevent information loss in exchanges between systems with different levels of model granularity, and interoperability preserves design intent information in mapping between different systems with different semantics.

The principles outlined have been used in the development of STEP translators that permit the satisfactory exchange of a limited class of CAD models between two different systems. The geometric coverage and types of parametric information exchanged are admittedly only a subset of what will be required for full practical translators, but the main objective of the work has been to provide a proof-of-concept test of the exchange of construction history CAD models with parameterization and constraints. Not all problems encountered have been fully overcome. However, it must be kept in mind that after the initial publication of Edition 1 of STEP in 1994 several years of experience were required before exchanges of boundary representation models became reliable. The exchange of procedural or construction history models is a new departure for STEP, and a comparable period of development must be expected.

Some recently developed STEP resources were used in defining the hypothetical application protocol described earlier. Together with earlier parts of the STEP standard, Parts 55 and 108 allow the transfer of parameterized procedural model representations in which some types of information are represented explicitly and others implicitly. Part 111 is used for the capture and representation of design features. The first two of these documents are already published as new parts of STEP, while Part 111 is in the ISO publication process at the time of writing. This research used development versions of all three documents that differ slightly from the final versions.

The APIs of commercial CAD systems are not primarily intended as an interface for the exchange of full parametric models. For that reason, it cannot be guaranteed that 100% of the model definition in the sending system can be successfully transferred to the target system. Even circular translation from a given system into the STEP format and then back into the original system may suffer loss of completeness, because some information in the original model may only exist implicitly and not be under the designer's control. We cannot therefore expect perfection in the present state of the art. However, the present paper makes recommendations for achieving the maximal possible information transfer, and it is believed that, subject to the general acceptance of some limitations, useful practical translators can be implemented that will realize the business advantages spelled out in [12]. For data exchange between CAD systems with similar data structures, the use of direct translators may be more effective (though their use has accompanying disadvantages), but for dealing with more general transfers the use of a neutral exchange medium such as ISO 10303 is strongly favored on all counts.

Future research will include the data exchange of user-defined features and feature-based assemblies between different CAD systems. This will involve models containing explicit constraints in 3D space. An ontological approach will also be adopted for the semantic mapping of modeling elements between CAD systems, based on the methodology outlined by Patil et al. [31].

DISCLAIMER

Certain commercial software systems are identified in this paper. Such identification does not imply recommendation or endorsement by the National Institute of Standards and Technology (NIST); nor does it imply that the products identified are necessarily the best available for the purpose. Further, any opinions, findings, conclusions or recommendations expressed in this material are those of the authors and do not necessarily reflect the views of NIST or any other supporting US government or corporate organizations.

REFERENCES

[1] ISO 10303, *Industrial automation systems and integration – Product data representation and exchange – ISO 10303:1994.* International Organization for Standardization (ISO), Geneva, Switzerland. Note: the ISO catalogue is online at http://www.iso.ch/cate/cat.html – search on 10303 for a listing of parts of the standard.

[2] Jon Owen, *STEP: An Introduction* (2nd ed.), Information Geometers, Winchester, UK, 1997.

[3] Michael J. Pratt, *Introduction to ISO 10303, the STEP Standard for Product Data Exchange,* ASME J. Computing and Information Science in Engineering, Vol. 1, 1, 102-103, 2001.

[4] John MacKrell, *Exchanging Product Design Data: Business Benefits of the Collaboration Gateway,* CIMdata, http://www.CIMdata.com, April 2004

[5] ISO 10303-55, *Industrial automation systems and integration – Product data representation and exchange: Integrated generic resource: Procedural and hybrid representation,* International Organization for Standardization, Geneva, Switzerland, 2005.

[6]   ISO 10303-108   *Industrial automation systems and integration – Product data representation and exchange: Integrated application resource: Parameterization and constraints for explicit geometric product models*   , International Organization for Standardization, Geneva, Switzerland, 2005.

[7]   ISO 10303-111,   *Industrial automation systems and integration – Product data representation and exchange: Integrated application resource: Elements for the procedural modelling of solid shapes*   , International Organization for Standardization, Geneva, Switzerland, 2007.

[8]   Yan Wang,   *Constraint-enabled Design Information Representation for Mechanical Products over the Internet*, Ph.D thesis, University of Pittsburgh, 2003.

[9]   Michael J. Pratt, *Extension of the STEP Standard for Parametric CAD models* , ASME J. Computing and Information Science in Engineering, Vol.1, No. 3, 269-275, 2001.

[10]   Akihiko Ohtaka, ISO TC 184/SC4/WG12 White Paper N295, *Parametric Representation and Exchange: A Sample Data Model for History-based Parametrics and Key Issues*   , January 1999.

[11]   Hong Gu, Thomas R. Chase, Douglas C. Cheney, Thomas T. Bailey, Douglas Johnson, *Identifying, Correcting, and Avoiding Errors in Computer Aided Design Models which affect Interoperability* , ASME J. Computing and Information Science in Engineering, Vol. 1, No. 1, 156-166, 2001.

[12] Michael   Stiteler, *Construction History And ParametricS: Improving Affordability through Intelligent CAD Data Exchange* , CHAPS Program Final Report, Advanced Technology Institute, 5300 International Boulevard, North Charleston, SC 29418, USA, January 2004.

[13] Ari   Rappoport, *An Architecture for Universal CAD Data Exchange* , in Proc. 2003 ACM Solid Modeling Symposium, Seattle, WA, USA, pp. 266-269, ACM Press, June 2003.

[14]   ISO 10303-203, *Industrial automation systems and integration – Product data representation and exchange: Application protocol: Configuration controlled design of mechanical parts and assemblies*   , International Organization for Standardization, Geneva, Switzerland, 1994.

[15]   Christoph M. Hoffmann and Robert Juan, *EREP: An Editable High-level Representation for Geometric Design and Analysis* , in Geometric Modeling for Product Realization, P. R. Wilson, M. J. Wozny and M. J. Pratt, eds., North-Holland, 1993.

[16]   Chia-Hui Shih and Bill D. Anderson,   *A Design/Constraint Model to Capture Design Intent*, in Proc. 1997 ACM Solid Modeling Symposium, Atlanta, GA, USA, ACM Press, June 1997.

[17]   Akihiko Ohtaka, ISO TC 184/SC4/WG12 White Paper N189, *Parametric Representation and Exchange: Preparatory knowledge about history based parametric model*   , August 1998.

[18]   Bernie Bettig and Jami J. Shah, Derivation   *of a Standard Set of Geometric Constraints for Parametric Modeling and Data Exchange* , Computer-Aided Design, Vol. 33, 17-33, 2001.

[19] ISO   10303-42, *Industrial automation systems and integration – Product data representation and exchange: Integrated generic resource: Geometric and topological representation*, International Organization for Standardization, Geneva, Switzerland.

[20]   Michael J. Pratt, *Extension of STEP for the Representation of Parametric and Variational Models*, in CAD Systems Development (D. Roller and P. Brunet, eds.), Proc. Intl. Workshop on CAD Tools for Products, Schloss Dagstuhl, Germany, Sept. 1995; Springer-Verlag, 1997.

[21] Guk-Heon Choi, Duhwan Mun and Soonhung Han, *Exchange of CAD Part Models Based on the Macro-Parametric Approach*, International Journal of CAD/CAM, Vol. 2, 13-21, 2002.

[22] Duhwan Mun, Soonhung Han, Junhwan Kim, Youchon Oh, *A Set of Standard Modeling Commands for the History-based Parametric Approach*, Computer-Aided Design, Vol. 35, 1171–1179, 2003.

[23] Michael J. Pratt, Bill D. Anderson and Tony Ranger, *Towards the Standardized Exchange of Parameterized Feature-based CAD Models*, Computer-Aided Design, Vol. 37, 1251-1265, 2005.

[24] Michael J. Pratt, *A New ISO 10303 (STEP) Resource for Modeling Parameterization and Constraints*, ASME J. Computing and Information Science in Engineering, Vol 4, No. 4, 339-351, 2004.

[25] Alfredo Pérez and David Serrano, *Constraint Based Analysis Tools for Design*, in Proc. 1993 ACM Solid Modeling and Applications Symposium, Montreal, Canada, pp. 281-290, ACM Press, 1993.

[26] Reiner Anderl and Ralf Mendgen, *Parametric Design and its Impact on Solid Modeling*, in Proc. 1995 ACM Solid Modeling Symposium, Salt Lake City, UT, USA, ACM Press, 1995.

[27] Steven Spitz and Ari Rappoport, *Integrated Feature-Based and Geometric CAD Data Exchange*, in Proc. 2004 ACM Solid Modeling and Applications Symposium, ACM Press, 2004.

[28] Christopher M. Hoffmann and Ku-Jin Kim, *Towards Valid Parametric CAD Models*, Computer Aided Design, Vol. 33, 81-90, 2001

[29] Jami J. Shah and Martti Mäntylä, *Parametric and Feature Based CAD/CAM: Concepts, Techniques and Applications*, John Wiley & Sons, 1995.

[30] V. Capoyleas, X. Chen and C. M. Hoffmann, *Generic Naming in Generative Constraint-based Design*, Computer Aided Design, Vol. 28, 1, 17-26, 1996.

[31] Lalit Patil, Debasish Dutta and Ram Sriram, *Ontology-based Exchange of Product Data Semantics*, IEEE J. Automation Science & Engineering, Vol 2, 213-225, 2005.

www.ingramcontent.com/pod-product-compliance
Lightning Source LLC
Chambersburg PA
CBHW080604060326
40689CB00021B/4931